PROFESSIONALISM IN PRIMARY TEACHING

Sara Miller McCune founded SAGE Publishing in 1965 to support the dissemination of usable knowledge and educate a global community. SAGE publishes more than 1000 journals and over 800 new books each year, spanning a wide range of subject areas. Our growing selection of library products includes archives, data, case studies and video. SAGE remains majority owned by our founder and after her lifetime will become owned by a charitable trust that secures the company's continued independence.

Los Angeles | London | New Delhi | Singapore | Washington DC | Melbourne

GLENN STONE

PROFESSIONALISM IN PRIMARY TEACHING

Learning Matters
A SAGE Publishing Company
1 Oliver's Yard
55 City Road
London EC1Y 1SP

SAGE Publications Inc.
2455 Teller Road
Thousand Oaks, California 91320

SAGE Publications India Pvt Ltd
B 1/I 1 Mohan Cooperative Industrial Area
Mathura Road
New Delhi 110 044

SAGE Publications Asia-Pacific Pte Ltd
3 Church Street
#10-04 Samsung Hub
Singapore 049483

First published 2022

Library of Congress Control Number: 2021942045

British Library Cataloguing in Publication Data

A catalogue record for this book is available from
the British Library

Editor: Amy Thornton
Senior project editor: Chris Marke
Marketing manager: Lorna Patkai
Cover design: Wendy Scott
Typeset by: C&M Digitals (P) Ltd, Chennai, India

ISBN 978-1-5297-6109-2
ISBN 978-1-5297-6108-5 (pbk)

CONTENTS

ABOUT THE EDITOR AND AUTHORS

ABOUT THE EDITOR

Dr Glenn Stone is a principal lecturer in education and coordinator for the undergraduate primary teacher training programme at University of Chichester. His research interests include teacher education and teacher professionalism.

ABOUT THE AUTHORS

Dr Linda Cooper is the programme coordinator for Education Studies at the University of Chichester. She also teaches history and social justice education across the ITT programmes. She publishes in the fields of primary history teaching and educational technology.

Kirstie Hewett is a senior lecturer in education at the University of Chichester and school improvement specialist at the University of Chichester Multi-Academy Trust. Her research interests centre around the professional learning of initial and early career teachers, and children's development in spoken language, reading and writing.

Debra Laxton leads the Early Years education provision at University of Chichester. Her particular research interests are attachment theory and the role of the key person, resilience and working with vulnerable families.

Gary Parkes is a former head teacher and is now a senior lecturer in education and assistant lead coordinator for the undergraduate training programme at the University of Chichester. His research interests include school leadership and the role of assessment in learning.

Dr Susannah Smith is a senior lecturer in Education at the University of Chichester. Her research interests focus on the socio-cultural influences on children's reading, the links between reading and identity, children's literature, and the explicit and implicit teaching of values and virtues in primary schools.

Jo Tulloch is a senior lecturer in education on the undergraduate and postgraduate primary teacher training programme at University of Chichester. Her research interests include the pedagogy of teacher presence in classroom practice and the reading and writing for pleasure agenda.

Dr Deborah Wilkinson is a senior lecturer in education and coordinator for the postgraduate primary teacher training programme at University of Chichester. Her research interests include how questions can be used to deepen learning in primary science and how teacher confidence impacts on teaching choices.

INTRODUCTION

GLENN STONE

This book emerged from the recognition that early career primary school teachers are joining a highly complex and valuable profession. Primary teaching is complex as the professional role encompasses so much more than the immediate work of delivering lessons to children. Primary teachers are connected through their professional relationships with children, school-based colleagues, the school community and external agencies. Their work is situated in complex structures which are governed by professional frameworks and focused on outcomes for the children, the school and wider societal expectations. They must achieve these outcomes in ways that are morally acceptable, in keeping with values that underpin the profession, the individual school and the individual teacher. Their professional development grounds them in knowledge of the full range of subjects taught, and they must also keep up to date with evidence-based practices for these subjects. Beyond classroom teaching, they have professional duties for safeguarding, health and safety and more. Therefore, an effective primary teacher is not just one who can teach phonics or primary geography successfully, but someone who is fulfilling the valuable, professional expectations of wider society. Primary teaching is a professional role, and this book is designed to support early career teachers in understanding that role.

The term 'early career teacher' has been used throughout this book to encompass those in initial teacher education and the early part of their career. Primary teachers in their early career will meet the Core Content Framework when carrying out initial training and the Early Career Framework in their induction period. They also need to meet the Teachers' Standards. This book has been written with those documents in mind. However, it does not seek to serve as a guide for passing the Standards or working through the frameworks. Instead, the book offers ways of thinking about the professional role of the primary school teacher and the importance of professionalism in primary teaching. As such, the book is particularly relevant when considering:

- Standard 8 of the Teachers' Standards (Fulfilling wider professional responsibilities);

- Part Two of the Teachers' Standards (Personal and professional conduct);

- Professional Behaviours of the Core Content and Early Career Frameworks.

Additional aspects of the Teachers' Standards and Core Content/Early Career frameworks are also mentioned where relevant.

Early career teachers, including student teachers and those working through induction, need to make sense of their professional identity and have a secure understanding of professionalism in order to navigate the complexities of primary teaching and their role as a teacher, inside and outside the classroom. However, no-one joins the teaching profession without having personal first-hand experience of teachers and teaching. Most people who have encountered the English education system in childhood would have spent twelve years in continuous education before embarking on a programme of further education. These personal experiences of education in childhood cannot be separated from the way that we view professional scenarios. In addition to childhood experiences of schooling, primary teachers may draw upon other aspects of their personal identities, such as race, ethnicity, culture, faith, religion, social class, gender. Personal and professional identities are therefore entwined and come together as primary teachers make sense of their role and responsibilities.

Professionalism may be seen as something that is socially constructed. Professionalism transcends different occupational groups, each with their own constructions of professional standards, professional behaviours and professional networks. People who engage with professionals will also have their own conceptions of what constitutes professionalism. There may be an appreciation for the professional response of an employee in a call centre, just as much as there may be appreciation for the professional opinion of a doctor of medicine, depending on what a person needs in any given context. Within primary education, professionalism can be discussed in terms of the government's professional standards; a head teacher's professional expectations of their staff; children's right to be protected within professional frameworks; professional dialogues with parents and carers; and more. In each case, what constitutes professionalism can be understood as something that has been socially constructed.

This book does not need to be read cover-to-cover, but there are some chapters that are designed to be read together in order to provide a broader picture for the issues that are discussed. The following chapter map may help readers navigate their way through the book:

Chapter 1 introduces ideas about professionalism and provides a starting point for early career teachers to think about their identity as a professional primary school teacher. The chapter establishes the importance of professionalism in primary teaching, along with the key professional considerations of trust, competence and autonomy.

Chapter 2 builds on the first chapter by considering the importance of values in primary education and connects this to primary teachers' professionalism. It links early career teachers' personal values with professional values and virtues, including expectations around fundamental British values in English schools.

Chapter 3 explores professional presence. Through practical suggestions, early career teachers are invited to consider how they can develop their presence and how this supports their professional role. It considers strategies for building presence and factors that may impact professional presence in the classroom.

Chapters 4 and 5 look at professional behaviours and professional relationships respectively. When the Core Content and Early Career frameworks discuss professional behaviours, much of the content relates to relationships. However, there are additional behaviours that teachers need to be cognisant of, particularly in order to uphold Part Two of the Teachers' Standards. As such, these dual chapters build a picture of the ways in which a primary teacher can demonstrate professionalism both through the way they act and the way they interact with colleagues, pupils and the school community.

Chapter 6 explores professional networks. This is a fairly recent area of professional practice in primary education, yet has become necessary as the teaching profession moves towards being more evidence-based. The importance of developing professional networks is explored and early career teachers are signposted towards the different types of networks that can be accessed for professional development. **Chapter 7** can be read alongside Chapter 6, as it builds on the ideas of networking but shows the opportunities for networking online. Alongside the many benefits of developing a professional profile online, the chapter also explores some of the challenges. In doing so, early career teachers are invited to consider their online identities and the importance of upholding public trust when engaging with social media and online communities.

Chapters 8 and 9 come together to build a picture of the professional frameworks and expectations placed upon primary teachers. The first of these chapters argues why it is important for teachers to follow professional frameworks and introduces some of the local and national frameworks that primary teachers work within. The final chapter focuses on the frameworks of accountability in greater depth as this is an area that early career teachers are often unfamiliar with, yet the consequences for those who cannot meet expectations is significant.

Running throughout the book is the golden thread of subject knowledge. It is unfortunate that some lay people still consider primary school teachers to be mere facilitators of gluing, colouring and painting. While arts and crafts are an important part of a child's education, and creations in their primary years are emblematic of their age, the role of the primary teacher is far more significant. Those who seek to trivialise the role have little understanding of the professional knowledge and skills that is required to be successful. Primary teachers teach across a range of subjects and so require broad subject knowledge. In order to raise their status as professionals, primary teachers need to be clear about why subject knowledge is important, how it builds their professionalism and how it can connect them to the broader professional community. As such, these aspects are explored across several chapters within this book.

Each chapter uses a number of features. The classroom links feature is one that enables readers to think through aspects of their teaching practice. Assignment links allow readers to think about ways of applying the content of the chapter to relevant assignments that may be part of initial teacher education programmes. The theory focus feature places a spotlight on theory or research, and connects ideas within the chapters. Similarly, critical questions invite readers to think carefully about different ideas as they work through the text. These features are designed to help navigate each chapter.

The authors of this book are passionate about developing professionalism in primary teachers. Their expertise in schools and higher education underpins the arguments made. As lecturers in initial teacher education they understand the importance of being gatekeepers to the profession and raising the status of primary education. It is hoped that this book will support those on their professional journey. Welcome to the teaching profession.

1

WHY IS IT IMPORTANT FOR PRIMARY TEACHERS TO DEVELOP A PROFESSIONAL IDENTITY?

GLENN STONE

KEY WORDS: AUTONOMY; COMPETENCE; IDENTITY; PHILOSOPHY; SUBJECT KNOWLEDGE; TRUST

INTRODUCTION

Why is it important for primary teachers to develop a professional identity? This chapter aims to answer this question by setting out some of the key considerations for primary teachers working as professionals. Initially, this chapter will explore the concept of teacher identity and what it means to be a professional. It goes on to explore why early career teachers may want to develop a personal philosophy of education and develop their subject knowledge for teaching. It is then argued that trust, competency and autonomy are facets of professionalism that are worthy of exploration by early career primary teachers. Throughout the chapter readers are invited to reflect on their developing professional identity.

DEVELOPING A PROFESSIONAL IDENTITY

It is commonplace for the primary school year to begin with teachers getting to know their pupils through some form of 'all about me' activity. Activities may include: children drawing a coat of arms to represent themselves; children bringing in artefacts from home for a show and tell; and pupils writing a postcard to share what they did over the summer holidays. Teachers will also use this opportunity to share their own hobbies, favourite things, or summer holiday. These early 'all about me' activities happen because identity matters. Yet, identity is not simply a list of likes and dislikes that can be shared on a colourful primary school display; an individual's identity is complex, multifaceted and shaped by a range of cultural, religious, social and emotional influences. As Beijaard (2019) states:

> Learning or developing a teacher identity is imbued with and fuelled by many aspects that are primarily personal, such as one's own biography, aspirations, learning history, and beliefs about education. Add to this the hopes, dreams, and ideals that students bring with them to teacher education.

> (Beijaard, 2019: 3)

Just as we hope to have a window into our children's identity through the 'all about me' activity, it is important for teachers to interrogate their own identity so that they can think about: how their own life history shapes their teacher identity; how they hope to be perceived as a teacher by others; and how they may fit within the shared identity of primary teachers as a professional group.

CLASSROOM LINKS WHAT PART OF ME IS ON SHOW?

Take a piece of paper and divide it into two. On one side draw yourself at home. Label this to show your personal characteristics. Think about how you see yourself and how others may describe you. On the other side of the paper, draw yourself as the teacher you want to be. Again, label this with characteristics. Now see how many of the words feature on both sides. Are there parts of your personality or identity that you would rather keep hidden from the 'professional' image or are the two pictures and sets of labels the same?

Through the activity above, you should have begun investigating your professional and personal identity. There may be aspects of your identity that are shared in both spaces. For example, a primary teacher who is a keen sportsperson outside of school will inevitably exude confidence and passion when teaching physical education. Thus, their professional identity as a teacher is connected to their personal identity. Indeed, extra-curricular clubs in school are often a window into the passions and interests of individual teachers that run these activities. However, there may be aspects of a teacher's identity that they want to remain personal and hidden from their children. This is more challenging and raises questions about the personal and professional self.

Collective identity is also something that early career teachers need to think critically about. If a school workforce is made up of teachers who have similar cultural, social and educational experiences, then the school's approach to curriculum, assessment and pedagogy may benefit from this consistent view of education. However, it may also mean that the school is resistant to change or new ideas. Approximately, 15 per cent of primary school teachers are male and 11 per cent of primary school teachers are from minority ethnic backgrounds (DfE, 2020b). This means that most children will encounter white female teachers for the majority of their formative years. A lack of diversity in the workforce of schools can also result in systemic issues that may go unnoticed or not tackled. A contemporary example of this is the Black Lives Matter movement that shines a light on the structural inequalities within broader society. The complexity of this topic demands more than simple solutions, but it is possible to see how schools that fail to portray black role models in discussions of history, or accurate representations of geography, will perpetuate these inequalities. Although *repositioning of curriculum will pose challenges for a teaching force that is predominantly white* (Race, 2020), the necessity to evaluate the curriculum will resonate with many teachers, but only if they are able to engage critically with their own identity first. Primary teachers, who are integral to helping shape a young person's worldview, need to recognise how their own identity helps or hinders this worldview.

How important is professional identity for primary teachers' effectiveness?

THEORY FOCUS CONNECTING TEACHER IDENTITY WITH TEACHER EFFECTIVENESS

A significant study of teachers' lives by Day et al. (2007) connects teacher effectiveness with identity. The longitudinal study, carried out with 300 teachers in 100 primary and secondary schools, recognises that there are variations in teachers' work and lives that impact on a range of factors inhibiting or enabling teacher effectiveness. They conceptualise the personal, professional and situational dimensions of teacher identity. Emotional and cognitive investment is required for effective teaching, and teachers draw upon personal and professional experience, knowledge and skill to achieve this. Where teachers are able to maintain a positive sense of their identity they are also likely to have a positive sense of well-being and agency. However, stability in teacher identity can fluctuate over time. There are many reasons why a teacher could fluctuate between different states of stability. For example, a teacher may suffer a personal crisis or may be faced by a new professional scenario, such as a change in policy or different pupil dynamic in a classroom. Where teacher identity becomes unstable the impact of professional and personal support is associated with the teacher continuing to be effective. Sometimes instability can lead to new ways of working, or an evaluation of existing practices that are needed. However, an unstable identity is likely to lead to ineffectiveness if it is long-lasting or if the personal and professional support is not there. As a result, teachers need to manage their identities by seeking the support they need and working through personal or professional challenges in order to maintain effectiveness.

The research findings by Day et al. (2007) highlight the importance of teacher identity. Effectiveness may be determined by an alignment of the personal, professional and situational. If a teacher feels that they 'fit in' with a school it is likely that these aspects will be aligned. If personal experiences, professional expectations and the situational context are not aligned, then it is easy to see why this would be unsustainable for the teacher in the long run, and how this could impact on long-term effectiveness. For this reason, it is important for candidates to study the school website, visit a school and get a feel for the school culture before applying for any teaching post.

WHAT DOES IT MEAN TO BE A PROFESSIONAL?

The word 'professional' and associated terms such as 'professionalism' are open to a plethora of interpretations. At its worst it can be a disciplining device (as in, 'you have not behaved professionally'), but far better is an association with high standards and public trust. Professionalism should also concern itself with promoting altruism over economics (Freidson, 2001). The goal of primary teaching is not to make money, but to help change society. This is not an argument for keeping primary school teacher salaries low; rather it is a principle for understanding that motivations for decision-making in educational settings should not be based on pecuniary interests, but instead on the ethical and altruistic purposes of education.

┌── CRITICAL QUESTION ───
│
│ How do professional teachers help society?
│
└──

People who are altruistic tend to think of others before themselves. Primary school teachers are not motivated to join the profession because of the extrinsic reward of their salary, but an intrinsic reward that comes from shaping the lives of young children. When interviewing candidates for teacher education programmes, in answer to the question 'Why do you want to become a teacher?' the response often follows, 'Because I want to make a difference.' When considering other professional occupations, including those where extrinsic rewards are more incentivising, there is a similar value of altruism. For example, medical professionals are primarily concerned with saving lives and have long been associated with the Hippocratic Oath, an ethical code that commits them to this cause.

Altruism is a good starting point for thinking about professionalism, but it is not sufficient on its own. After all, a person who volunteers in a charity shop is making a valuable and principled contribution to society but may not be described as being a member of a profession. Therefore, teachers may be classed alongside other professional occupations as being distinct from other roles in society that may be equally deserving of recognition. This idea is supported by Carr (2000) who argues that in order for human beings to flourish, we need access to things beyond that which we need for basic survival. Education, a legal system and healthcare are not essential for survival, but undoubtedly enable a civilisation to flourish. Within these domains, professional occupations can be easily found. Furthermore, it is *significant that the kind of services that professionals are in business to provide have increasingly come to be regarded as human rights* (Carr, 2000: 7). These professional services are also contested widely, vary geographically and culturally, and are politicised in recognition of their importance within a society. Returning to the volunteer in the charity shop, we can quickly see that however altruistic their motivations, their work is not the subject of societal scrutiny or contention and the service they provide is not seen as a human right.

┌── CLASSROOM LINKS ───
│
│ In some occupations, it may be easy to articulate the reason why you may do the job. For some peo-
│ ple in some jobs it is purely financial (often in low-income jobs where someone works in order to pay
│ the bills). For many occupations, the reason for doing the job goes beyond the financial. Professional
│ occupations, in particular, connect their work to broader societal needs.
│
│ Consider your professional identity and motivations for teaching when answering the following
│ questions:

- In schools where budgets are restricted, how will you compensate for a lack of resources?

- If a child has a learning need but without additional funding, how will you break down barriers in order to ensure the child is able to make progress?

- To what extent can you close the attainment gap between low- and high-income families?

- What training needs and support do you require in order to teach in ways that do not marginalise any group of pupils?

Primary school budgets could always be greater, but a strong primary teacher can mitigate for this. Beyond initial teacher education, primary teachers should connect to research and evidence to support their development. It is crucial that a professional teacher does what they can to enable all children to make good progress.

Consideration of motivations for teaching may be linked to an individual's values. For further discussion of professional values and teaching, see Chapter 2 of this volume.

HOW ARE COMPETENCY, TRUST AND AUTONOMY LINKED WITH PROFESSIONALISM?

Evetts (2009) signposts trust, competency and discretion as being integral to definitions of professionalism. A primary teacher's competence as a professional is demonstrable on a daily basis. Children will respond negatively if their teacher is not prepared for a lesson; head teachers will become concerned if a teacher lacks subject knowledge; parents will raise the alarm if their children are not making progress. The competent teacher is more likely to be trusted to make their own decisions. However, a teacher who lacks competence will require more support and direction, thus eroding their autonomy, and it may take time to earn complete trust from all stakeholders.

CRITICAL QUESTION

Why is it important for primary teachers to develop their subject knowledge?

In the past decade, the importance of teachers' subject knowledge has received greater attention, and teachers are more likely to be seen as lacking competence when their own subject knowledge is weak. Policy drivers such as the National Curriculum and Ofsted's focus on curriculum design have placed a further spotlight on the value of subject knowledge as part of teacher identity. In primary schools this can sometimes be a greater challenge as, unlike secondary, there is not the same scope for specialising in one subject. Furthermore, there have been concerns that there is a *growing and worrying trend towards widespread cultural and educational deficit on the part of many primary trainees ... who seem nowadays to be deficient in the most basic general knowledge of culture and history* (Carr and Skinner, 2009: 152).

Traditional definitions have emphasised an esoteric knowledge as being integral to professional work as opposed to other forms of work (Freidson, 2001, explores this in greater detail). Shulman's (1987: 8) seminal work on teacher subject knowledge identifies a range of categories of the knowledge base. Specialist to teaching is the *pedagogical content knowledge … [that] represents the blending of content and pedagogy in an understanding of how particular topics, problems or issues are organized, represented and adapted to the diverse interests and abilities of learners, and presented for instruction.* When forming a professional identity for primary teaching, this pedagogical content knowledge requires expertise and time to develop. Primary teachers may take an interest, or have passions, for one subject or more, but they must also possess sufficient subject knowledge in a range of areas. Therefore, knowledge of healthy eating is as important as knowledge of the Stone Age and it is necessary to know how best to teach healthy eating in science and how best to teach the Stone Age in history.

The pursuit of knowledge should be seen as integral to a teacher's professional identity. How could a teacher competently secure a child's development within a subject if their own subject knowledge is insecure? Furthermore, how can a teacher use their professional discretion to make autonomous pedagogic choices if they lack the subject knowledge to base their decision-making upon? If primary teachers are unable to impart knowledge, how does this affect public trust?

Helsby and McCulloch (1996) propose that teachers should determine for themselves how they teach, develop and negotiate their work using their curriculum knowledge at a classroom level. However, we know that the work of teachers is subject to national and local frameworks that may reduce capacity for autonomy. For example, the National Curriculum, local assessment frameworks and a school's own teaching and learning policy will impact teachers' pedagogy, what is taught and how taught content will be assessed. Such national and local frameworks have increased over many decades so it may be that there has not been a golden age of autonomy since the 1960s. Nevertheless, professional autonomy remains important for teachers (Day, 2020) and is significant to teacher identity. Primary school classrooms, in particular, can be unpredictable environments when we consider the maturity and development needs of the children that inhabit them. As such, early career teachers need to develop skills in reflexivity in order to develop autonomous responses to the children in their classrooms. However, this is only possible if a teacher has strong subject knowledge to underpin the dynamic decision-making that is necessary.

CLASSROOM LINK ACCESS TO TEXTBOOKS

An early career teacher tells their mentor that they are least confident in teaching grammar. The mentor suggests the use of a textbook scheme to support the teaching in the classroom. On first glance at the textbooks, the early career teacher believes that they are uninspiring. However, when given to the children, the teacher notices that most children are able to work through the first few pages with relative ease. A few children find the textbooks more challenging. After a couple of weeks, the children meet a grammatical term that they had not visited before and the teacher is not sure what the term is, so the children are encouraged to skip the page and move onto something else.

Consider the scenario above. What messages are there within this for the professionalism of the teacher? How has the textbook helped and hindered the learning? What could the teacher do to make the learning better?

The use of high-quality textbooks for teaching can reduce teacher workload and also provide a coherent sequence of lessons that aids the learning process. However, some may argue that reliance upon published schemes and textbooks erodes teacher autonomy. This would be true if schemes and textbooks are followed to the letter; yet, this is rarely the case. In the primary sector, while there is a plethora of commercial resources that teachers can draw upon, there are few textbooks schemes that would work for every single child. The Core Content and Early Career frameworks refer to sharing and making use of well-designed textbooks. The quality of the textbook is therefore of paramount importance and professionals need to develop the evaluative skills to establish which textbooks are going to maximise impact in classroom. As such, the skilled and autonomous teacher will need to know: which textbook to choose; when to introduce the textbook; how to adapt their instruction in order to maximise the effects of the textbook; formative assessment strategies to support a child who finds it difficult to access the textbook; and more. Therefore, textbooks only erode teacher autonomy if the teacher uses them to replace their professional discretion instead of using such resources to complement their teaching.

Developing professional competence takes time. Evetts (2009) points out that the 'professional' musician does not limit their practice but instead dedicates countless hours to perfecting an instrument. This professional work-ethic can be problematic for primary teachers who have been found to work on average 50 hours per week (DfE, 2019b). In some cases, teachers may feel compelled to spend time completing tasks that are not directly related to teaching (Stone, 2020). Therefore, in pursuit of professionalism, primary teachers should consider how time is spent. The development of subject, curricular and pedagogic knowledge is necessary for the competent and professional teacher. The development of bureaucracy may be better suited for those that seek to be professional administrators.

Through both initial teacher education and their early careers, teachers should gain greater confidence and competence. Student teachers will only be awarded Qualified Teacher Status in England if they have demonstrated that they have the competence to become a teacher. Competent teachers are then trusted to carry out their duties. Every day, parents entrust their children to schools; school communities trust that children are safe in school; wider society trusts that primary schools are providing the requisite standard of education that is needed. Without this trust the primary school would cease to function appropriately. For early career teachers it is necessary to build trust between pupils, parents, colleagues and the wider school community. Indeed, the professional Teachers' Standards make clear, *Teachers uphold public trust in the profession and maintain high standards of ethics and behaviour, within and outside school.*

THEORY FOCUS TRUST AND TEACHING

Trust may be seen as a hallmark of professionalism, particularly when considering the ethical implications. Brien (1998) makes a connection between trust and acting ethically:

A person can also promote trust in themselves by showing that she is a reliable, conscientious, honest person who 'does the right thing'. In other words, by acting ethically or being a member of an institution, whose members are known to be ethical actors, and who police such entry standards. Conversely, we do not trust people who fail to abide by the norms of a society in

(Continued)

(Continued)

> which we have an investment, be it a society or a sub-group, such as a profession, or who are members of a sub-group known to be ethically dubious.

(Brien, 1998: 400)

From Brien's definition, we can see that it is important for the individual teacher to demonstrate that they can be relied upon to behave and act ethically. It is also important for the broader profession to uphold hold public trust through their collective reputation. Indeed, schools are a microcosm of society and therefore reflect the norms of the society. If the public felt that schools were working in ways that were discordant to the values of society then public trust would soon erode. It is therefore essential for the teaching profession to promote ethical practices and sustain rigorous entry standards in order to ensure that any parent can entrust their child to the school.

Another way of thinking about trust is to consider one's professional reputation. Competent teachers will build a professional reputation within a school and its community.

CASE STUDY

Mr Forbes is an early career teacher in Year 6. He has not yet found his feet and has been struggling with behaviour management. Every day he tries the same strategies but they are not working. He realises that he spends a lot of lesson time telling off certain children and is becoming further behind in delivering the curriculum. The children go home to their parents each day and say that they have done little learning. Some children have expressed concern about the behaviour of other children in their class. A couple of parents ask to speak with Mr Forbes but he is worried about what they are going to say so he claims to be too busy. The parents begin to exchange stories on the playground and soon Mr Forbes is portrayed as an incompetent teacher. One parent posts some unpleasant comments about Mr Forbes on a local social media page. Parents in Year 5 are beginning to become concerned that their children may have Mr Forbes next year.

What could Mr Forbes do differently? From whom could he seek advice or guidance to ensure that trust is not eroded between himself and the parents? In what ways could trust between himself and other professionals in the school break down if things don't improve?

In the scenario above, it is shown how a teacher's reputation can become tarnished, resulting in a breakdown of trust between a teacher and some parents in the community. If Mr Forbes is an isolated case, the school will preserve a more positive reputation. However, if misbehaviour in Year 6 escalates, or if other teachers in the school are unable to foster positive behaviours for learning, then the school reputation will be adversely affected. The community may no longer feel that they can entrust the school with the education of their children. Developing a professional reputation takes time. However, as explored earlier in the chapter, it is essential for early career teachers to seek support and guidance when things are challenging. Also, of importance is the ability to build relationships between teachers, pupils, parents and the wider community. This aspect of professional trust will be explored in more detail in Chapter 4 of this volume.

HOW IS TEACHER IDENTITY LINKED TO THEIR PERSONAL PHILOSOPHY FOR EDUCATION?

The question 'What is education for?' is often explored by student teachers, either as a formal or informal component of their initial teacher education. It is not the intention here to explore the philosophy of education, but instead to connect personal philosophies with professionalism.

First, it is worth noting that teachers are not the only people seeking answers to questions about the aims of education. Politicians and policy-makers, most of whom have little practical experience in the classroom, will have their own philosophies of education, often with ideological perspectives underpinning this. Parents will also consider the aims of education, particularly in relation to how and where they want their children to be educated. At the ballot box, the general public may have a view on how education should be shaped and, consequently, politicians are mandated to devise policy that takes education in one direction or another. So where does a teacher's personal philosophy of education fit into the overall picture? Biesta et al. (2015) argue that in order to achieve greater agency as a teacher it is important to develop a range of beliefs about teaching, including personal beliefs about the purposes of education. Agency in this sense is similar to the discussion of autonomy above.

CRITICAL QUESTION

How does a teacher demonstrate their personal philosophy?

A teacher's personal philosophy can be contextualised by considering school behaviour management policies. For example, behaviourist theories often underpin such policies in the way that they emphasise rewards and sanctions, and have clear guidance on processes for managing recalcitrant children. However, primary teachers are often keen to build relationships and understand a child's misbehaviour, thereby adopting humanistic, relational responses as part of their behaviour management repertoire. A teacher who does not accommodate such humanistic approaches is likely to have a different interpretation of the school behaviour policy. This does not mean that the strategies will be any more or less successful, but rather that personal philosophy, or beliefs, underpin a teacher's agency and is demonstrated through their pedagogical choices.

THEORY FOCUS DEVELOPING A PERSONAL PHILOSOPHY AS A PROFESSIONAL

Personal philosophies take time to develop and may not be matured through initial teacher education or even the early stages of a teacher's career. Bérci (2006) theorises a staircase through which professionalism is developed alongside a personal awareness of the professionalisation process. It is suggested that educators begin as *practical conformists* (p. 58) where they use a lot of intuition

(Continued)

(Continued)

and are not yet stable in their professional identity. As the teacher ascends the analogous staircase, they will eventually reach the final step: *authentic philosophical professional* (p. 59). Those that have acquired an authentic philosophical professional identity are able to appreciate the plurality of perspectives in education by taking on board other people's personal philosophies; they are more confident in justifying their own decision-making:

> *Their identity as teachers and as persons has unified. Though they may have to submit to some conventional and external norms of behavior, they no longer diverge from their basic philosophical framework without reasoned justification. The importance of the pursuit of deep self-knowledge is paramount and they recognize that such pursuit is never-ending. They consciously choose teaching, understand the profession as an integral part of who they are as persons and use the profession to create a life that encompasses their own beliefs of what is right and useful.*
>
> (Bérci, 2006: 60)

Bérci goes on to argue that at different times, a person could ascend or descend the analogous staircase. In other words, it is unlikely that someone will be permanently working in an authentic philosophical professional state. A whole range of contextual factors can influence teacher identity and it may be necessary to retreat to the practical conformist stage before working back up the staircase again.

As Bérci (2006) theorises, personal philosophies and professional identities evolve over time. To support this, it is useful for early career teachers to seek opportunities for philosophising about the aims of education, both individually and in consultation with other primary teachers.

CHAPTER SUMMARY

Why is it important for primary teachers to develop a professional identity?

Although identities and personal philosophies of education take time to develop and mature, it is a worthwhile process to reflect upon who you want to be as a teacher and why you want to teach. To support your developing professional identity, this chapter has:

- considered what it means to be a professional;
- explored the importance of competence, autonomy and trust.

ASSIGNMENT LINKS

Many assignments on teacher education programmes will invite you to put across your own philosophy of education. For example, you may be asked to write about effective practice in a subject, or your approach for curriculum design. Your reflections within these assignments will be underpinned by your developing teacher identity. In other words, the way that you eventually teach will be grounded in personal motivations, personal beliefs and philosophy of education. As such, it may be appropriate to conclude assignments by connecting your ideas to your professional identity. In doing so, it may be helpful to consider: how you want to be perceived as a teacher; how effective teaching practice upholds public trust; and what your particular teaching approach says about your personal philosophy of education.

FURTHER READING

To consider the importance of agency within the professional identity of teachers, it is worth reading the following text:

Biesta, G., Priestley, M. and Robinson, S. (2015) The role of beliefs in teacher agency. *Teachers and Teaching*, 21(6): 624–40

In this text the authors explore the complexity of agency and how it can be understood and realised within the work of teachers. The authors make a compelling case for greater understanding of the purposes of education and connect this to the value of agency.

2

WHAT ARE PROFESSIONAL VALUES AND WHY ARE THEY IMPORTANT?

SUSANNAH SMITH

KEY WORDS: FUNDAMENTAL BRITISH VALUES; PROFESSIONAL VALUES; SCHOOL VALUES; VALUES; VIRTUES

INTRODUCTION

This chapter will discuss the place of values in the teaching profession. The values of individual teachers will be considered and you will be encouraged to identify the values that are most important to you. Teachers are required to maintain high standards of ethics and behaviour, within and outside school, and you will be encouraged to reflect on potential challenges you might face, particularly regarding your behaviour outside school. Schools are required to publish their ethos and values on their websites and you will be encouraged to think about the type of school in which you would like to work. Finally, you will be introduced to fundamental British values since teachers are required to promote these in school.

WHAT ARE VALUES?

In a discussion of professional values, it is helpful to begin with a definition of values. At the simplest level, values are the beliefs which guide and motivate the attitudes and actions of individuals and of societies. Values determine what is important to an individual, the sort of person they want to be and how they want to behave:

> [Values are] *principle and fundamental convictions which act as justifications for activity in the public domain and as general guides to private behaviour; they are enduring beliefs about what is worthwhile, ideals for which people strive and broad standards by which particular practices are judged to be good, right, desirable or worthy of respect.*
>
> (Halstead and Pike, 2006: 24)

Values therefore dictate an individual's private and public actions, and they are ideals for judging what is good and right. Halstead and Pike (2006) continue that examples of values are justice, equality, freedom, fairness, happiness, security and truth.

Virtues are related to values and they are the personal qualities or dispositions of an individual. They are concerned with a person having a good character and include qualities like truthfulness, generosity, courage, loyalty and kindness. Halstead and Pike (2006: 24) also discuss attitudes which they define as *acquired tendencies or predispositions to behave in a predictable manner*, which include openness, tolerance, respect and freedom from prejudice. Values, virtues and attitudes are related and overlap, but the distinction between them will be helpful later when we examine the values which individual schools define as those most important to their ethos.

CLASSROOM LINK WHAT IS IMPORTANT TO YOU AND WHERE HAVE YOUR VALUES COME FROM?

From this list of values and virtues, choose the five that are most important to you:

charity, confidence, courage, generosity, hard work, honesty, kindness, loyalty, modesty, perseverance, protecting the environment, resilience, respect for others, responsibility, tolerance.

Why did you choose these five? Your values are influenced by the family you grew up in, the friends you chose and the society in which you live. Can you make links between the values you chose and the values of your family, friends and wider society?

Finally, consider how the values influence your practice in the primary classroom.

The study of ethics, or moral philosophy, is concerned with what is good for individuals and society and with how people make decisions and lead their lives. It includes the study of how to live a good life, good and bad moral decisions, and what is right and wrong. Therefore, discussions about values and virtues are at the heart of moral philosophy. Virtue ethics, deontology and utilitarianism are all key theories in the study of ethics and will be explained in the following section.

WHAT ARE INDIVIDUAL TEACHER VALUES?

It stands to reason that since teachers are individuals who have different influences on them, individual teachers will prioritise different values. There are probably many values which will be common to all teachers; for example, honesty, kindness and respect. It would be hard to imagine a teacher who did not value honesty in their private life and in their classroom. There may, however, be some values which differ in importance between teachers. This may be due to an individual's personal beliefs and passions. For example, a teacher may be passionate about climate change and may live out the value of protecting the environment by eating a vegan diet and restricting the number of children they have. Differences in the importance of different values may also be due to an individual's religious belief. For example, a teacher may prioritise the value of charitable giving which they believe to be fundamental to their religious belief. There could even be instances where an individual teacher's values are in conflict with those of a school: for example, regarding beliefs about same sex relationships. A teacher might not be supportive of same sex relationships and this could put them in conflict with a school which prioritises the value of respect for others.

The values which are prioritised by individual teachers are important because teachers are role models for pupils; teachers live and model their values to children. The Initial teacher training core content framework (DfE, 2019a: 9) recognises that *Teachers are key role models, who can influence the attitudes, values and behaviours of their pupils.* Teachers will reinforce those values which are most fundamental to their beliefs in their classrooms, and this will be communicated to the pupils. For example, if a teacher prioritises the values of perseverance and resilience they are likely to highlight and reward behaviours which demonstrate these values, giving the pupils the message that these values are important. The values that the teacher promotes will therefore influence the children's own moral development.

In the definition of values at the beginning of the chapter it was noted that values guide an individual's private behaviour and activity in the public domain. The Teachers' Standards (DfE, 2011) state that teachers should *maintain high standards of ethics and behaviour, within and outside school.* High standards of behaviour are thus expected *outside school,* as well as inside. There is likely to be little debate that teachers must demonstrate high standards of behaviour in school, but it is interesting to further consider the ethics and behaviour of a teacher outside school. Consider the following case studies which highlight some of the issues raised.

CASE STUDY ROSIE

Rosie is in her first year of teaching. She lives in the town where she grew up and works in a local primary school. At the weekend, Rosie likes to go out with her friends. They often spend the evening drinking in local pubs and sometimes go on to a nightclub.

Discussion: In this scenario, what does it mean to *maintain high standards of ethics and behaviour*? Is there a limit on the amount Rosie should drink? Would it be acceptable for her to take recreational drugs?

On one occasion, Rosie drank more alcohol than usual and started to feel unwell. She went to the toilets where she sat on the floor with a bottle of water. One of her friends took a photo of her and posted it on social media. When she got to school on Monday morning, Rosie was called into the head teacher's office. The parent of one of the children in her class had seen the photo on social media, taken a screenshot and emailed it to the head teacher.

Discussion: High standards of ethics and behaviour are expected *outside school.* What does this mean for a teacher's private life? Does being a professional mean that there are limits on what a teacher can do in their own time? How do you feel about having to behave in a certain way outside school?

In order to further consider the case study of Rosie it is helpful to refer to key theories in the study of ethics, particularly virtue ethics and deontology.

THEORY FOCUS VIRTUE ETHICS

Virtue ethics originated in ancient Greek philosophy, particularly from the work of Aristotle (384-322BCE). It focuses on the individual rather than the action: on the virtue or moral character of the person carrying out the action. It provides guidance as to the sort of characteristics and behaviours a good person should seek to attain. Virtue ethics is concerned with a person's whole life and a good person is one who possesses and lives the virtues. This presupposes a common set of virtues for all human beings and this poses a challenge since there are differences in lists of virtues that have been written at different times. The traditional list of 'cardinal virtues' was prudence, justice, fortitude and temperance. A more contemporary philosopher suggested justice, fidelity, self-care and prudence as virtues for the modern day (Keenan, 1996). There is, however, no general agreement on what the most important virtues are and it may be that any list of virtues needs to be relative to the culture in which they apply.

If Rosie's case study is regarded through a virtue ethics lens, her behaviour has certainly fallen short. Her behaviour would not be considered to be of high moral character and she would have fallen short on virtues such as prudence, temperance and self-care.

THEORY FOCUS DEONTOLOGY (NON-CONSEQUENTIALISM)

Deontology, or duty-based, ethics is also based on what people do and not on the consequences of their actions. The key philosopher associated with deontology is Immanuel Kant (1724-1804). Individuals should do the right thing because it is the right thing to do; an action cannot be justified by showing that it produced good consequences (hence deontology is non-consequentialist). Deontologists live by moral rules, such as it is wrong to kill, it is wrong to steal, it is wrong to tell lies and it is right to keep promises. While this may appear morally right, someone who follows deontology should always do the right thing even if it produces a bad result. Kant gave the example that it is always wrong to tell a lie, even if the lie saved a friend from a murderer. Deontology does, therefore, provide certainty, but it can lead to action which reduces the overall happiness of the society.

Through a deontological lens, Rosie has also fallen short. Her behaviour is not the morally right thing to do and she is not being a good role model for her pupils. Campbell (2003) argues that the ethical teacher is, by necessity, an ethical person and that a teacher with integrity would apply the same moral code to their everyday life and to their classroom. If a teacher acts differently in their private and professional lives they would need to have a clear justification for this based on a well thought through ethical position.

CASE STUDY HAMZA

Hamza is passionate about climate change. When he was at university he was a climate activist and he got involved in a protest where he chained himself to a tree to stop it being cut down to make way for a new ring road. Since becoming a teacher Hamza has reduced his activism but he did recently attend a protest march in London and during the march he was arrested for a breach of the peace.

(Continued)

(Continued)

Discussion: Where would you draw the line between Hamza having strong beliefs about an issue and the actions he should engage in to highlight the issue? Is it acceptable to attend a protest march? Is it acceptable for a teacher to take action which leads to being arrested?

In order to further consider the case study of Hamza, it is helpful to refer to another key theory in the study of ethics: utilitarianism.

■ THEORY FOCUS UTILITARIANISM (CONSEQUENTIALISM) ■

Utilitarianism is a branch of consequential ethics and focuses on the consequences of actions. It is associated with philosophers such as Jeremy Bentham (1748-1832) and John Stuart Mill (1806-1873) and is the belief that the actions of individuals and institutions can be measured by the capacity to promote the greatest happiness of the greatest number. Bentham argued for the principle of utility: that human decisions are founded on maximising pleasure and reducing pain. Whether an action is right or wrong depends on the result of the act and the individual should choose the actions which maximise human well-being and good consequences. While this may seem desirable, it means that no action is inherently wrong; it depends on the result of the action. Taken to extreme, this could include murder. A utilitarian might say that killing one person is justified if it saves the lives of five other people.

Utilitarianism states that whether an action is right or wrong depends on the result of the act and the individual should choose the action which maximises human well-being and good consequences. Hamza could argue that his actions were justified since the potential result of his action – government policy to reduce climate change – would be a good consequence for many people, including the children he teaches, and hence maximise human well-being.

These case studies highlight the complexity of a teacher's individual position. There are often 'grey' areas rather than 'black and white' answers as to how teachers should behave, particularly outside school. Trainee and newly qualified teachers need to think carefully about their behaviours and the consequences of their actions. This is what is referred to as 'professional values'; once you are a teacher, your values have to reflect the fact that you are a professional and part of this is having to demonstrate high standards of ethics and behaviour in and out of the work environment. Carr (2000: 25) suggests that *someone may be judged unfit to practise professionally because, despite their possession of relevant theories and skills, they lack appropriate* values, attitudes or motives (emphasis in original). He believes that an individual could have values and attitudes which make them unsuitable to be a teacher.

___ **CLASSROOM LINK IS THERE ANY CONFLICT BETWEEN YOUR PRIVATE LIFE AND YOUR PROFESSIONAL ROLE?** _____

Can you identify any values, beliefs or behaviours you have which might cause conflict between your private life and your role as a teacher?

Do you need to modify any of your behaviours? How do you feel about this? Do you need to develop a set of 'professional values' which you are comfortable to live by, both in and out of work?

WHAT ARE SCHOOL VALUES?

All schools are legally obliged to include a statement of their values and ethos on the school website (DfE, 2021b). A search of school websites shows that frequently occurring values include the following:

- achievement/academic success

- creativity

- enjoyment

- friendship

- helping others

- honesty

- independence

- kindness

- perseverance

- resilience

- respect for others

- responsibility

- teamwork/working together

- tolerance.

In the first section of this chapter, it was noted that Halstead and Pike (2006) distinguish between values, virtues and attitudes. It can be seen that what schools refer to as their values actually include a mixture of values (e.g. honesty), virtues (e.g. resilience) and attitudes (e.g. respect for others). In fact, there are also overlaps: for example, honesty can be a value and a virtue. When discussing school values, the term 'values' will be used as an umbrella term for values, virtues and attitudes.

The first question that might be asked is 'Who chooses the school values?' The values of an individual school may be chosen by the senior leadership team of the school, led by the head teacher. This may or may not be done in consultation with other stakeholders of the school, including governors, teachers, non-teaching staff, parents and pupils. This is one way in which a new head teacher can 'make their mark' on a school. If they change the school values this can give an indication of the type of school they wish to lead. If the school is part of a multi-academy trust, it is likely that the trust will have central values which are adopted by all schools in the trust.

The second question that might be asked is 'How are the school values chosen?' The values chosen are likely to be influenced by the vision the head teacher or the head of the trust has for the school. The values chosen might be influenced by a religious standpoint: for example, Church of England or Catholic schools are likely to have values which are reflected in the religion. The values chosen may also be influenced by the socio-economic context of the school. Smith and Smith (2013) found that schools in lower socio-economic areas were more likely to promote the values of perseverance and resilience, whereas schools in higher socio-economic areas were more likely to promote the values of charitable giving and helping others. Schools tend to choose values which they believe to be important for and relevant to the children in their school.

The third question that might be asked is 'How are the school values promoted?' Schools will usually have their values displayed, around school as well as on their website. The school values will be often be encouraged through recognition and rewards for displaying the values. Many schools have some form of 'celebration assembly' and, as well as recognising high-quality work, these assemblies will often recognise children who have displayed the school's values. Many classrooms will have a reward system whereby pupils receive a reward when their behaviour demonstrates one of the school values in action.

CLASSROOM LINK PROMOTING SCHOOL VALUES

What strategies have you seen in schools for promoting the school's values? Do you think these are successful? Do you think children internalise the school's values and display them in their behaviour?

Think about how you would like to promote school values in your classroom. How you do this might have an impact on the ethos in your classroom. For example, if you highlight examples of kindness to others with a recognition or reward, your classroom is more likely to become a place where children feel safe and cared for.

Before leaving this section, it is valuable to think about the school's values from the child's perspective. For many children, developing the school values will not be problematic. However, for some children there may be differences between the values which are encouraged in school and the messages they receive at home.

CRITICAL QUESTION

What happens if school values are in conflict with the messages a child receives from home?

Schools can set their values and encourage them to be enacted in school. However, what happens if these values are different from the messages a child is getting at home?

<hr/>

CASE STUDY MARK

Mark is a pupil in Year 3 (aged seven) who keeps getting into trouble for fighting in the playground. He often comes in the classroom after breaktime or lunchtime upset, having got into a fight, and it takes time for Sam, the class teacher, to resolve the issues and be ready for the next lesson to start. Sam has tried many strategies with Mark, including reminding him of the school value of being kind to others and imposing a sanction when he breaks this by fighting; rewarding him when he has a breaktime without getting into a fight; and talking to him to try to understand what might be going on which would explain why he is getting into fights. At parents' evening, Sam brings up the issue with Mark's parents and his dad's response is *I tell him, you hit them before they hit you.*

This explains Mark's behaviour. The message Mark is receiving from home is in conflict with the school value of being kind to others. How do you think it feels to Mark to have different behaviour expectations on him at home and in school?

If you were Mark's class teacher, what would you do? How would you help Mark modify his behaviour in school without undermining his family?

WHY IS IT IMPORTANT FOR INDIVIDUAL TEACHER VALUES AND SCHOOL VALUES TO ALIGN?

This section will bring together the sections on an individual teacher's values and school values. Teachers need to ensure that there is a match between their personal values and the school values. Stone (2012: 131) points out that *prospective teachers need to determine their teaching values and match these to a compatible school.* Essentially, teachers are likely to be much happier if their personal and professional values align. Teacher well-being is important for the school and the pupils, as well as for the individual teacher; teachers are likely to be much happier and more productive at work if they are in a school where they feel that there is a match between their personal values and the school values. Where there is a good match between values, teachers are more likely to feel part of a wider team where all staff are working together towards a shared vision, and this can engender feelings of being valued and high levels of job satisfaction.

<hr/>

CRITICAL QUESTION

What sort of school would you be happy working in?

Consider the values of the two schools below. What might the values tell you about the school? Do you think you would be happier working in one school more than in the other one? These schools are fictitious but the values are all taken from a selection of real schools.

(Continued)

(Continued)

School 1: Chestnut Green Primary School

High expectations, no excuses! We aim to improve behaviour and learning by developing the following values in our pupils:

academic success

exemplary behaviour

responsibility

confidence

independence.

School 2: Four Bridges Primary School

We live the following values as we grow and learn together in our community:

love

friendship

happiness

honesty

compassion

charity.

Have a look at websites of primary schools local to you and read the school ethos and values on the website. Find a school with values you believe would align with your own. Is there a school you would not want to work in?

You should always visit a school before deciding whether to apply for a job in the school. There may be a mismatch between the values the school says it promotes and the reality in the school.

Of course, teachers may need to accept jobs for pragmatic reasons: for example, the job was the only one they saw advertised within a 30-minute drive from their home. However, teachers can change jobs and if they are not happy at a school they should consider if the reason for this is a mismatch between their values and the school values and whether a change to a school where there is a closer match might be a beneficial move.

Schools can be caught between conflicting pressures which impact on the delivery of their values. Head teachers and teachers want children to thrive and be happy at school and their values are often holistic ones, concerned with developing the whole child. However, schools are judged on their academic results, and head teachers and teachers often feel pressure to focus on achieving high academic standards. This may manifest itself in curriculum time being focused on the aspects of the curriculum which will be assessed, such as English and mathematics, at the expense of more creative and expressive subjects, such as art and music. It can, therefore, be a challenge for head teachers and teachers to ensure that the pressure to achieve high academic results does not dominate over values focused on pupils' wider development and well-being.

WHAT ARE FUNDAMENTAL BRITISH VALUES?

Before leaving this chapter, it is important to discuss fundamental British values because, since 2014, it has been a requirement that schools promote these values. The fundamental British values are:

- democracy;

- the rule of law;

- individual liberty;

- mutual respect and tolerance of those with different faiths and beliefs.

These values were first set out by the government in the Prevent strategy which is part of the government's counter-terrorism strategy (Her Majesty's Government, 2011). It is interesting to note that in the extensive Prevent strategy these values only appear in a definition of extremism:

> Extremism is vocal or active opposition to fundamental British values, including democracy, the rule of law, individual liberty and mutual respect and tolerance of different faiths and beliefs.

> (footnote, p. 34; glossary of terms, p. 107)

In the Prevent strategy, reference is also made to *fundamental values* of *universal human rights, equality before the law, democracy and full participation in our society* (foreword, p. 1) and to *mainstream British values* which are given as *democracy, rule of law, equality of opportunity, freedom of speech, and the rights of men and women to live free from persecution of any kind* (para. 6.60, p. 34). It is interesting to note that the list of *fundamental British values* from the glossary were adopted for schools to promote rather than other lists of values which appear elsewhere in the strategy; no explanation is provided for this.

In 2014, the DfE published guidance on promoting fundamental British values in school within the spiritual, moral, social and cultural (SMSC) curriculum with the aim of ensuring that young people leave school prepared for life in modern Britain. Schools are inspected on their effectiveness in promoting fundamental British values as part of the 'Education inspection framework' (Ofsted, 2019). Under the heading of 'Personal development', inspectors make a judgement on the extent to which *the provider prepares learners for life in modern Britain by … developing their understanding of fundamental British values* (Ofsted, 2019: 11, para. 28).

CLASSROOM LINK FUNDAMENTAL BRITISH VALUES

What does it mean to promote fundamental British values? What might this look like in schools?

'Promoting fundamental British values as part of SMSC in schools' (DfE, 2014) describes the understanding and knowledge expected of pupils and includes examples of actions schools can take to develop this. It includes the following: age-appropriate material on how democracy and the law works; promoting a school council with members voted for by the pupils; and holding mock elections during the time of general or local elections.

What might promoting fundamental British values look like in classrooms? Can you think of practices that you could implement in your classroom?

As an example, many teachers include the children in setting 'classroom rules' at the beginning of the year, involving them in a democratic process.

As well as schools being required to promote fundamental British values, teachers are required to 'not undermine' them. The Teachers' Standards (DfE, 2011: 14) includes the following statement:

Teachers uphold public trust in the profession and maintain high standards of ethics and behaviour, within and outside school, by: not undermining fundamental British values, including democracy, the rule of law, individual liberty and mutual respect, and tolerance of those with different faiths and beliefs

CRITICAL QUESTION

Can you think of any ethical difficulties you might have with promoting and not undermining fundamental British values?

You are required not to undermine fundamental British values which includes the rule of law. Have you ever committed an offence? This would include getting a speeding ticket.

What do you think should happen to teachers who do break the law? Does it depend on the nature of the offence? Which offences should/should not exclude teachers from the profession? Look back at the case study of Hamza. Do you think he should be excluded from teaching after being arrested for a breach of the peace during a legal protest march?

The requirement for schools to promote fundamental British values and for teachers to not undermine them has been critiqued by academics. The first critique centres on the fact that, in promoting the fundamental British values from the Prevent strategy, teachers are required to have a part in the government's counter-terrorism strategy.

Gilroy (2018: xi) points out that teachers *find themselves, whether they realise it or not, a key element of the government's anti-terrorist strategy*. Lander (2016: 274) refers to counter-terrorism as having *invaded the professional pedagogic space* and believes that the government's counter-terrorism strategy and the Teachers' Standards should not be conflated since this amounts to using *teachers as instruments of the state.* The second critique focuses on the word 'British', and that the implication the values are wholly British can be regarded as inherently racist. Lander (2016: 275) points to the racism inherent in referring to 'British' values since it encourages notion of the 'other' and creates a notion of citizens where some really belong (the indigenous majority), some can belong (those of minority ethnic heritage who have assimilated or integrated) and some do not quite belong and are tolerated up to a point (the Muslim 'other'). Elton-Chalcraft et al. (2018: 346) question whether it is possible to have a shared understanding of fundamental British values given the diverse nature of Britain and note that different teachers interpret the vales differently, that some teachers have a limited understanding of fundamental British values and that some teachers draw on fundamental British values to reinforce an 'us' and 'them' standpoint which could be described as 'veiled racism'.

CONCLUSION

This chapter has provided a discussion of the place of values in the teaching profession. You have been introduced to definitions of values and virtues, and to key theories in the study of ethics. You have learnt about the requirements for teachers to maintain high standards of ethics and behaviour, within and outside school, and for schools to have a public statement of their ethos and values. You have been introduced to fundamental British values and the requirement for schools to promote these and teachers not to undermine them. You have been invited to consider your personal position in relation to these discussions, including identifying the values that are important to you, any challenges you might face, particularly regarding your behaviour outside school, and you have been encouraged to spend time thinking about the type of school in which you would like to work.

▬ CHAPTER SUMMARY ▬

Why is it important for primary teachers to understand their professional values? Primary education evolves with both local and national policy initiatives. As part of their professional identity, primary teachers who know their professional values will be able to make sense of unfamiliar contexts and work through contemporary issues in education. This chapter has considered:

- how values guide and motivate the attitudes and actions of individuals and of societies;

- the distinctive nature of virtues as part of developing a good character;

- the professional values that result in high standards of ethics and behaviour that teachers have to demonstrate in and out of the work environment;

- how schools are legally obliged to have a statement of their ethos and values and to publish this on their website;

- how primary teachers can ensure that there is a match between their personal values and the values of the school in which they work;

- it is a requirement for schools to promote fundamental British values and for teachers not to undermine them.

■■ ASSIGNMENT LINKS ■

Your assignments will reveal your values. Sometimes you are asked about these explicitly (e.g. write an essay that reflects your philosophy for the teaching of primary maths); other assignments will be more nuanced with regards values. For example, you may need to write a reflection on behaviour management observed in a setting. When reflecting, your values will come into play. They will under-pin what you believe is right or wrong in any given situation. As such, when writing any assignment, it is worth considering how your own values influence the way you interpret source material. This criticality will help improve the quality of your work.

■■ FURTHER READING ■

Jackson, P., Boostrom, R. and Hansen, D. (1993) *The Moral Life of Schools*. San Francisco: Jossey-Bass

The authors conducted an ethnographic study in Chicago which focused on the direct and indirect influence that teachers and schools have on the development of moral values in children and young people. The research highlights the ways in which moral considerations permeate all aspects of school life and are part of the ethos of the school.

3

HOW DO PRIMARY TEACHERS DEVELOP THEIR PROFESSIONAL PRESENCE?

JO TULLOCH

KEY WORDS: PRESENCE; 'WITHITNESS'; CONFIDENCE; SYNCHRONY; IDENTITY; PERFORMANCE; PERCEPTION; ENERGY

INTRODUCTION

In this chapter we will explore what it means to have teacher or classroom presence and how that can be gained, developed and maintained. We will begin by asking what key pedagogies, attributes and skills are required to have strong teacher presence and will go on to find out more about the strategies that teachers can practise to support the development of this in the classroom.

WHAT DO WE MEAN BY 'TEACHER PRESENCE'?

This vague term 'teacher presence' has no obvious clear definition in pedagogical literature or in educational policy, yet often features as a developmental target for early career teachers, particularly in initial teacher education. A trainee teacher may be asked to: 'Develop your teacher presence.' In these situations, trainee teachers and maybe even more experienced teachers also are not always entirely sure *what* teacher presence is or *how* they should develop it.

Perhaps teacher presence as a concept is most easily comprehended when associated with our own childhood school experience. We can probably recall those teachers who would blend into the background in lessons or have little to no impact on the classroom environment or the children in it. We understand presence in this instance 'by its very absence' (Rodenburg, 2007). Similarly, we can also probably recall teachers who seemed to be able to walk into a classroom or assembly hall and immediately, with a flick of the fingers, a raised eyebrow or just by being there, captivate the children and hold their attention and engagement; these teachers just seemed to have the 'it factor' – 'teacher presence'.

CLASSROOM LINKS

Think back to a teacher you had in school, a teacher who stood out to you as having 'presence'. What were they like? How did they behave? How were they thought of? Were they funny, loud, calm? Did

(Continued)

(Continued)

they have particular strategies or actions that were effective? Were they the kind of teacher that had a reputation for being good/deserving of respect? Make a mental list of personality traits and behaviours that you think may have had impact on their presence. Consider what, if any, of these personality traits and behaviours you feel you would want to replicate in your own practice. Are there any traits that you would not want to replicate?

It seems clear that teacher presence is noticeable by the impact it has on the respect or reputation that a teacher has and, in turn, by the way a class responds to that teacher and the way that teacher is identified. It is therefore an important aspect of professional teacher pedagogy since it has this direct connection to effective classroom practice.

THEORY FOCUS BEING PRESENT

Terms such as 'mindfulness', 'alertness', 'awareness' and 'attentiveness' are more often used in rela-tion to philosophical or spiritual states of being, but these terms are also apparent in educational studies. Carol Rodgers and Miriam Raider-Roth in their seminal research on this subject define teacher presence as:

a state of alert awareness, receptivity, and connectedness to the mental, emotional and physi-cal workings of both the individual and the group in the context of their learning environments.

(Rodgers and Raider-Roth, 2006: 265)

They continue by identifying teacher presence as *bringing one's whole self to full attention so as to perceive what is happening in the moment* (Rodgers and Raider-Roth, 2006: 267). A central focus here is the idea that teachers can use their own personal qualities or energy (Rodenburg, 2007) to optimise their teaching practice so that their teaching is both effective and personally fulfilling. This means that the full awareness of the here-and-now, which is what presence is all about, encompasses and connects both the teacher's self – their core qualities – and the environment: what Meijer et al. (2009) define as the process of *being while teaching*. Rodgers and Raider-Roth discuss further that teacher presence is a *slow motion awareness* (2006: 271) and an open acceptance of the pupils in the class, free of judgement, exemplified with genuine interest and care in the pupils' learning and progress. Teacher presence also includes a degree of passion, not just for the subject matter, but also for learning itself; the energy and curiosity associated with this passion keeps teachers alert and engaged with the learner and the learning. Teacher presence is when their attention is not only on the learner but also simultaneously on the class, the environment(s) in which they are working, the next steps in learning for the individual and class, the creative and cross-curricular subject matter(s) at hand and the place and value of that subject matter in and to the larger society. For Rodgers and Raider-Roth, *presence is no small thing* (2006: 271).

In your own teaching practice, it is important to ensure that you are alert and attentive to the pupils and environment around you, a key element of teacher presence. Some practical ideas to support this would be to ensure that you are well hydrated and rested if you can. It is difficult to maintain a focus and attention in lessons when you are tired and dehydrated. It may also be a sensible idea to set a timer for your lessons so that you can give your full attention in the moment without losing complete track of time.

THEORY FOCUS PRESENCE AS ENERGY

Patsy Rodenburg, an acting teacher of great renown, focuses her teaching about presence on what she calls *circles of energy*. In her seminal text *Presence* (2007), she introduces the notion of the *first circle* being inward facing where the focus of your energy is on yourself and where the energy *falls back into you*. This position is manifested in an averted gaze and a body that is collapsed and disconnected. At its worst, a person in the first circle is hiding their presence away inside themselves. In the *third circle*, Rodenburg identifies that there is a generalised connection or pushing of energy outward but not specifically to a person or people. Words are spoken not to affect, but into space, in general and often too loudly. A person in the third circle may show this by a pushed-out chest and chin, presenting themselves forcefully into the space. It is in the *second circle* where Rodenburg sees that a person is fully present and in the moment. Here the focus is placed outside yourself, but words are spoken to affect another. *Circle Two* energy represents the perfect balance; it is the powerful, reciprocal energy of true connection, which focuses on a specific object or person and, crucially, moves in both directions, taking in and giving out. As a teacher - any role that requires presence - this is the circle to remain in. The physical representation of second circle presence in the body, breath and voice is full attentiveness, and aligns with openness and focus in the mind and heart; it is a state of readiness or alertness. Physically, the weight is on the balls of the feet, the spine is straight, shoulders are relaxed and the body actively forward, ready to engage. Most importantly, there is eye contact and a calm, deep and unrushed breath.

CLASSROOM LINKS

In your own teaching practice become aware of the circles of energy that you are working within. Are you inward focused, unable to hold the eye contact with your class and hunched in body posture? Or do you tend to raise your voice and push your physical presence into the classroom more forcefully to try and get attention? Consider how you can focus your energy into the second circle; allow your presence to be fully alert and focused on connection with the pupils in the class. Think about holding eye contact with the pupils and really listening to them when they speak.

WHAT UNDERPINS YOUR TEACHER PRESENCE?

CRITICAL QUESTION

Is teacher presence a natural, innate gift, or is it something that can be cultivated, practised and used - and, more importantly when training to be a teacher, something that can be taught and learnt?

Like many teaching characteristics, presence should be seen as a multifaceted professional quality which is in equal measure personal-, performance- and perception-related.

- *Personal:* presence is very much linked to a teacher's personality, sense of self and identity in the classroom: 'who you are' as a teacher.

- *Performance:* presence is about the way a teacher acts or functions in the classroom: 'what you do' as a teacher.

- *Perception:* presence is about how a teacher is perceived in the classroom or school environment, whether that is their status, experience or even reputation.

Figure 3.1 shows how these three facets in teacher presence can be explored in their own right, but are also intrinsically linked to each other in a reciprocal and influencing way; this will be explored in the rest of this chapter.

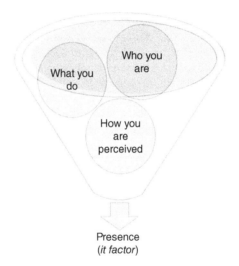

Figure 3.1   Facet funnel of presence

HOW IS TEACHER PRESENCE INFLUENCED BY WHO YOU ARE?

It would be an unfortunate situation indeed for initial teacher education if teacher presence was only an innate or natural ability since arguably that would limit the pool of necessary, keen and trainable potential classroom teachers. However, 'who you are', your personality or character, is viewed as important for teacher presence as this can and does impact on a teacher's behaviour and manner in the classroom. Teachers are often described by their pupils in relation to their personality or character: for example, 'she is very kind' or 'he is really funny' or 'they are always cross'.

However, whether authoritative, calm or humorous, any incongruence between the authentic personal identity and professional personality leads to a divided self (Meijer et al., 2009) and will diminish teacher presence. In this respect, early career teachers often hold their 'authentic' selves in reserve while training. They construct a teacher self, the image of whom, in their minds, their schools or initial teacher training institutions expect a teacher 'should' be (Goodson and Cole, 1994). Concerned that their authentic selves are not acceptable or appropriate, they try to be whom they 'should' be. When a teacher acts solely from an artificially constructed notion of who they should be they become remote or separate from themselves and presence becomes difficult. This distance between personal and professional selves can cause a tension which goes beyond the tension that naturally exists for new teachers that can undermine both trust in themselves and their pupils' trust in them. Amy Cuddy, in her work on presence, reiterates this, stating that when being inauthentic, verbal and non-verbal behaviours misalign and facial expressions do not match the words being said: *our postures are out of sync with our voices* (2015: 23).

CASE STUDY

One trainee teacher noted that on his practice he observed how pupils in a class could tell if a teacher was not being themselves and that this would impact negatively on a teacher's presence. If a teacher tried to be a certain way - for example, if they tried to be funny when that was not true to their character - then the children in the class would 'spot the fake'. This trainee teacher felt this was indicative of not having teacher presence.

Reflect on how you feel most comfortable when teaching. Are you regularly making jokes and telling funny stories with the class? Are you measured and considered in your practice? Do you think you have a bubbly and chatty teaching personality, or do you feel you have a quieter and more reflective one?

How would you feel if you were asked by a mentor or school leader to 'try and be more entertaining' or 'calm your personality down' in the classroom?

Whether we like it or not, personality does seem to impact on teacher presence in the classroom and being authentic, true to your personality or, as the case study puts it, being yourself, is a facet of this presence. At this early stage of the teaching journey it could be argued that early career teachers are still figuring out personal and professional identities (Trent, 2014); it could be too early to have a fully developed sense of identity as a teacher, or a sense of themselves with a professional identity, and this might impact on their own sense of teacher presence. If this is the case it is clear that 'who you are' as a teacher, your teacher identity or personality, is not something that is fixed in place but is evolving and flexible and will develop over time. Whether your authentic personality will change significantly or not is debatable, but what will grow and develop is your confidence as a teacher.

The understanding seems to be that with time and experience comes confidence, authority and ultimately presence; one trainee teacher summed this up by saying: *if you have got it from the start it helps, but you can learn it too.* To gain confidence in teaching and teacher presence it is important that different orders of knowledge are developed: good subject knowledge, pedagogic knowledge, knowledge of what the children are doing in the class at the time of teaching and also knowledge of the children beyond the time of teaching – their families, histories (in the class and beyond) and so on (Rodgers and Raider-Roth, 2006). Having secure subject knowledge for the lesson to be taught enables the teacher to demonstrate a stronger teacher presence. Being confident in what you are teaching frees you up to be more attentive to the needs of all learners and react and respond to situations as they arise. Your focus as a teacher is on the 'in the moment', present learning rather than becoming overly concerned with remembering the lesson plan. In the same way that an actor can improvise a role within a play when they have learnt the script fully, a teacher is able to do the same and demonstrate presence in the class and improvise in the lesson when they are secure in what they are teaching. In addition to self-confidence and secure subject knowledge, having a good knowledge of primary pedagogical approaches and teaching strategies supports teacher presence. Having confidence in behaviour management techniques, use of questioning and teacher modelling, for example, will enhance a teacher's presence in that they will be able to adapt their teaching to the needs of the pupils and manage class dynamics and the learning environment effectively. The ability to learn in the moment (Meijer et al., 2009) or, as one trainee teacher put it, to *roll with the punches* and be flexible within a lesson requires a confidence to be willing to make mistakes and learn from them.

CLASSROOM LINKS

Reflect on how your teacher presence is impacted on by the subject you are teaching. Think about how confident you feel when teaching your specialist subject compared with a subject that you are less familiar with.

- How can you prepare differently for a lesson you are less confident teaching?

- How will this ensure that your presence is still strong in those lessons?

- How confident are you to 'roll with the punches' in a lesson?

Teacher presence is often equated to enthusiasm or passion. Teacher enthusiasm or passion has been highlighted as a key element of effective, high-quality teaching, a desirable characteristic of good teachers and an essential ingredient of supportive classrooms. There is generally a widespread notion that the majority of teachers are passionate and enthusiastic about their job (Day, 2004), particularly as the conditions of the profession do not appear to be offering any other extrinsic motivation to encourage them. However, is teacher presence really synonymous with passion or enthusiasm? Isn't it perfectly possible that a teacher can be passionate and enthusiastic about teaching and about their pupils, but still not have that elusive quality of teacher presence and so be ineffective and lack inspiration?

CLASSROOM LINKS

Think about something you are passionate about (e.g. a film or show you have watched/a hobby/ book/activity). How would you encourage your friends or family to watch, read or try the activity you are promoting? How would your voice and body language show passion and enthusiasm? Presence has a lot to do with passion and interest; how will this impact on your teaching?

▬ THEORY FOCUS SYNCHRONY ▬

Amy Cuddy's work defines presence as 'synchrony' where the *various elements of the self - emotions, thoughts, physical and facial expressions, behaviours - must be in harmony* (Cuddy, 2015: 34) and 'comfortable' with each other. One needs to be true to one's own personality in order to be comfortable: comfortable in teaching and comfortable with being in front of the class. Cuddy observes that when someone is truly present, then they are able to work at an optimum, with a clear focus, stating:

> *When we are truly present in a challenging moment, our verbal and nonverbal communication flows. We are no longer occupying a discombobulated mental state simultaneously analysing what we think others think of us, what we said a minute earlier, and what we think they will think of us after we leave, all while frantically trying to adjust what we're saying and doing to create the impression we think they want to see.*

(2015: 22)

Arguably, this is exactly how a teacher needs to be in classroom practice, amid the challenge of the lesson; to have a clear uncluttered mental state is desirable. In order to achieve this, Cuddy controversially investigated how powerful body posture and movements influence positively a person's confidence for a task or presentation. Cuddy found that those who sat in the high-power expansive pose (superhero style pose) felt more powerful and confident and performed better in mock interviews than those who had not. Although Cuddy's work looked at ways that body power postures could help a person feel more confident and present, she warned that presence is not about pretending, but about building confidence and revealing the abilities you already have. Enthusiasm and passion are qualities that are very hard to fake; so, for Cuddy, to harness these qualities alongside the physical behaviours and facial expressions synchronously is to begin to demonstrate presence. When present, she asserts *speech, facial expressions, postures, and movements align. They synchronize and focus* (2015: 16).

▬ CRITICAL QUESTION ▬

What helps you have teacher presence?

So, it can be seen that teacher presence is in many distinct ways associated to who you are as a teacher – there is need for synchrony between your authentic self and your teacher self, your personality, confidence, passion and authority for presence to develop and thrive. This is not the whole picture though. Let us now consider how what you do and how you are perceived impact on your teacher presence.

Look at the largest circle in Figure 3.2. There are a number of factors that relate to what a teacher can do to impact on teacher presence. These are largely pedagogical practices that make up a teacher's professional work and therefore perhaps not surprisingly in this list. A good professional teacher will be expected to demonstrate all these. However, what is worth noting is that they are all aspects of teaching that can be learnt and developed over time and with training. If teacher presence as a concept feels out of reach for you as a teacher, then it may be worth focusing attention on some of these more practical and applicable professional skills in order to develop a teaching presence in the classroom.

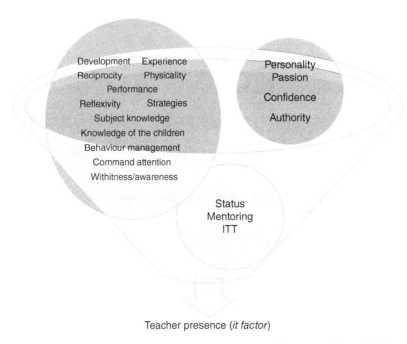

Teacher presence (*it factor*)

Figure 3.2   Expanded facets of presence

HOW IS TEACHER PRESENCE INFLUENCED BY WHAT YOU DO?

PHYSICALITY

Physical posture or stance – how you stand in front of the pupils or how you move around the classroom – clearly identifies an aspect of having a *noticeable presence* (Bruner, 1971). A teacher's posture (how they are standing) can give an unintentional message of being 'closed off' or 'open' to the pupils without the use of words. One trainee teacher observed they crossed their arms deliberately to indicate their *serious mode* and another discussed 'non-verbal communication' as a *big part of teacher presence*. As already mentioned, using power poses (Cuddy, 2015) has been proven to increase sense of confidence and keeping eye contact, as in the second circle of energy (Rodenburg, 2009), enables the teacher and pupils in the class to engage with each other more and demonstrate an interest in what each person is saying. A small hand signal or a 'look of the eye' helps in supporting teacher presence as the connection between the non-verbal aspect of teacher presence and the need to manage behaviour.

Try these physical actions to help focus on your physical stance and posture:

- have equal weight on both feet;

- stand tall (head like a ping pong ball);

- shoulders back;

- no tension in the arms;

- feet should be like anchors, rooting you to the floor;

- try some power poses – star shape/star jumps, stand like a superhero!

The pitch, tone and volume of the voice also impact on the teacher presence. Almond (2004, 2019) and Hart (2007) recognise the importance of developing the voice to support teacher presence, establishing voice coaching for trainee and experienced teachers. Constantly raising the voice to get attention or to manage behaviour, apart from putting tremendous strain on the vocal chords, serves also to diminish authentic teacher presence as the focus is on a forceful and stressful working environment.

CASE STUDY

One trainee teacher described a teacher who *changed their pitch as they moved around the room* or being able to say something in *a slightly different way … you could hear the seriousness in his voice.* Another Key Stage 1 teacher, in describing the way they used a countdown from 10 to 1 as a class management strategy, noted how the pupils in the class always seemed to respond to particular numbers in the countdown more than others. The numbers 4 and 7 seemed to be heard by the class clearer; the teacher realised that when she called these numbers the pitch of her voice dropped significantly and the pupils seemed to respond to the change to a lower pitch.

How often have you been teaching in the classroom and found that you have a sore throat or you have lost your voice by the end of the day? Could this be due to using your voice in a strained way or raising your voice too often?

What would happen if you began whispering or lowering your voice in the classroom? Give it a go and see?

Tension in any part of the body immediately has a constricting influence on the human voice. It is important to be aware of this and take time to consider some relaxation exercises before beginning a class; only when the body is relaxed can the voice be free and the mind fully creative. Try these exercises before a lesson as a way to relax the body and the voice:

- stretch: up, out, down, gently roll up;

- squeeze and tense the muscles in isolated body parts and then release the muscles;

- shake it out;

- with your head: push forward, push back, tilt left, tilt right, drop forward and recover.

Breath is the power of speech and understanding how this works is key for any teacher using their voice as a primary method of communication. Consider how, when nervous, the breath becomes shallow and rapid, speech can sound breathy and words can catch in the throat. To combat this, try these exercises to support your breathing.

- Floor breathing: locating the breath. As you breathe in and out, place your hand on the tummy and feel the tummy rise and fall – ensure you breathe from the diaphragm, not the shoulders.

- Breathe in through the nose for three, hold for three, out through the mouth for three.

- Swing arms for five (don't let shoulders rise).

Strong articulation is essential if you wish to communicate with the class clearly. If a pupil cannot hear what you are saying they will initially get frustrated, then lose interest and disconnect. Aim for a crispness of utterance and clarity of enunciation. Practise articulation with these exercises:

- practise phonics articulation;

- practise reading aloud poems and song lyrics;

- practise tongue twisters (e.g. *Whose pigs are these? Whose pigs are these? They are Mrs Potters, you can tell them by the trotters, and you find them in the peas*).

Modulation refers to the musical and variable qualities of the speaking voice, which include pitch, pace, inflection, volume, intensity and the use of pause. A well-modulated voice will always resonate over a monotonous one and will command attention more readily. Your voice must remain your own, do not try to imitate someone else's, you do not need to.

- Practise reading stories aloud using different voices.

- Vary your vocal range: whisper, high voice, low voice, roller coaster voice, etc.

THEORY FOCUS PHYSICAL PRESENCE

Any academic search on the term 'teacher presence' brings up an array of articles on the rise of 'invisible' or 'absent' presence of the teacher in virtual, online and distance learning, as opposed to the physical presence of a teacher in a real classroom (Hudson, 2008). The distinction here is the need for a noticeable physical presence. The noticeability of a teacher is what identifies that teacher as having teacher presence. Bruner (2009) suggests that to maintain interest and attention (a noticeable presence), 'dramatising devices' or 'dramatic aids' can be called upon - for example, use of posture and body language, gait, stillness, gesture (Almond, 2004; Tauber and Mester, 2007), physical relaxation, place of speech, quality of voice and speaking clearly (Almond, 2019). These devices or aids seem to place the notion of teacher presence into the field of performance.

PERFORMANCE

The experience of teachers agrees that *teaching is undeniably a performing art* (Lowman and Lowman, 1984: 11) and, as Tauber and Mester assert, *there is an educational foundation for using acting skills in the classroom* (2007: 423). Performing the role of teacher is, however, distinct from the strategy of a teacher performing 'in role'. It is also distinct from the act of storytelling or story reading in the classroom, although this does 'depend on presence' and demonstrates the skill many teachers have in dramatising a story with animation and enthusiasm, using a variety of tone and different voices. Both acting 'in role' and storytelling are part of the performance that a teacher gives; but it is the role *of* the teacher which is in itself an act or performance. Dr Mark Almond from Canterbury University carries out acting workshops with language teachers to develop their teaching presence. He states that *just as actors have a stage or screen presence, we as teachers can develop classroom presence by transferring certain skills from the stage to the classroom* (2004: 8).

If the notion of performing in the classroom fills you with dread, consider how important it is for teachers to express with the whole body, not just with verbal language, particularly when managing behaviour or communicating with pupils with English as a second language. Key areas to focus on with regard to expression are your face, eyes and hands. Hands are very useful to capture attention and to identify presence, but if they become too busy they will distract from the teaching. Open hands are usually symbolic of welcoming and approachable; closed hands or folded arms traditionally communicate a disinterest or a lack of intention to commit.

▬ CLASSROOM LINK ▬

Try some of these activities to help develop this non-verbal aspect of your presence.

Can you show these feelings using no words?

- Welcoming/warm
- Understanding
- Happy
- Stern
- Encouraging

Once mastered, use these non-verbal cues with your class and evaluate how effective they were at conveying your meaning.

'WITHITNESS'

The notion of 'withitness' (Kounin, 1970) can be seen as an aspect of teacher presence. It can be discussed in terms of having an awareness of what the children are doing and what is going on all over the classroom. It is the ability to have your eye on someone across the classroom to the point that you are everywhere, even though you are not everywhere. Rodgers and Raider-Roth (2006) called this being 'alive to the children'. It is important that a teacher is able to physically see all the children in the class – that is, to position themselves in places where this is possible; even if the teacher is sitting with one group, they should still be able to see the rest of the class. This physical presence is not only the teacher being aware of the class, but also the children in the class needing to have an awareness of the teacher at all times too. In order to develop withitness in the classroom space:

- don't be afraid to move (the teacher's desk/table is a barrier);

- move with confidence and purpose;

- don't get locked or become rigid;

- try not to jump around too much or be over-active;

- be calm and methodical in your movements.

HOW IS TEACHER PRESENCE LINKED TO THE WAY THAT TEACHERS ARE PERCEIVED?

There is a link between the situational aspects of school settings and teacher presence in the classroom. The more a trainee teacher is enabled in the situation, the more sense of presence they feel. This means it is important to be in the context or environment where perceptions will be formed: whether it is seen by their personality or character (who they are); whether it is in the way they behave or the strategies they adopt (what they do); whether it is the status they are given (how they are perceived); or whether it is the situations they are put in or filtered through. Presence will struggle to exist in hostile or untrusting situations (Rodgers and Raider-Roth, 2006), but in contrast a relationally healthy teaching–learning context will enhance and optimise the conditions required for a teacher's capacity to be present, for their focus to be on the in-the-moment teaching opportunities (Meijer et al., 2009; Rodgers and Raider-Roth, 2006).

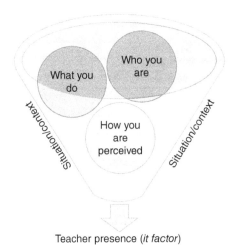

Figure 3.3 Expanded facets of presence filter

CASE STUDY

A trainee teacher recalled a school placement where they had been excited to be introduced to the class for the first time. It was a Year 6 class which had a reputation for being challenging. The class teacher introduced the trainee teacher as a student who had come to the school to learn all about teaching. The teacher went on to discuss with the pupils how frustrating it was to have a student in the class as there was so much work to do with SATS coming up and that there really was not any time to teach the student as well.

A different trainee teacher recalled how they were introduced on their school placement. The class teacher introduced the trainee as *This is Miss____ and she is going to be teaching you this term. I am really looking forward to learning new things from her.*

Has this ever happened to you? Reflect back on the way you have been introduced to a class on teaching practice.

How can you mitigate for a less than positive introduction to a class?

Consider how you can introduce yourself in a class - construct some introductory sentences such as *Hello, my name is Mr ... and I am going to be teaching you for some lessons this term* or *I am really looking forward to teaching you this week.*

In the above case study there are two very different approaches to the same situation. The first trainee teacher really struggled with establishing a teacher presence after that introduction, whereas the second trainee teacher had been gifted with an element of teacher presence from the outset in that she was already perceived to be a teacher.

WHAT ELEMENTS OF TEACHER PRESENCE CAN ACTUALLY BE TAUGHT AND LEARNT?

It is clear that particular subject knowledge and pedagogical and practical teaching strategies or 'techniques' that support or develop teacher presence can be taught and learnt either while in training, or through continuing professional development. One trainee teacher spoke about the fact that teacher presence was something they *learnt a lot more on placement rather than at university.* Being in the shared or 'figured' world of school enables trainee teachers to participate in the speech genres, social language, jargons and patterns of communication of being a teacher (Holland et al., 1998). The onus needs to be on developing core reflective practices (Korthagen, 2004) which would allow teachers to consider how practice is exemplifying teacher presence or not (Scharmer, 2016). It is important to be aware of what causes teacher presence and what constitutes teacher presence, and then reflect on that. In order for this to be effective one would need to know roughly what you are looking for as improvements will not be possible if you don't know what teacher presence is. Therefore, teacher presence is something that can be improved and developed, but it is important to have a clear and consistent conceptualisation of teacher presence between the early career teacher and others that are offering support (such as mentors).

For teacher presence to be effective it is necessary for there to be a positive relational element to the classroom. A teacher's effectiveness and authority are embedded in those relationships that they build with their pupils (Rodgers and Raider-Roth, 2006). Nel Noddings (2003) recognises the importance of reciprocity in developing teacher presence, particularly in terms of the teacher needing to foster a caring teaching and learning relationship. In a classroom where there is an authentic and respectful connection between the teachers and pupils, where they can bring their feelings, experiences, memories and hopes to one another, pupils can know that teachers are ready and available to participate in the learning journey knowing that they will undertake it well accompanied (Rodgers and Raider-Roth, 2006).

CHAPTER SUMMARY

What is professional teacher presence and how does a teacher develop this in their classroom practice?

Teacher presence is multifaceted and complex with three distinct aspects: that of 'who you are', 'what you do' and 'how you are perceived'.

To support your developing professional teacher presence, this chapter has considered:

- what it means to have teacher presence;
- how teacher presence can be developed;
- what strategies can support teacher presence;
- factors that impact on teacher presence.

ASSIGNMENT LINKS

If writing an assignment about behaviour management, it is important to consider how this will be influenced by teacher presence. Unpack what teacher presence is, using this chapter to help you, and connect it to the professional role of the teacher.

FURTHER READING

Meijer, P. C., Korthagen, F. A. and Vasalos, A. (2009) Supporting presence in teacher education: the connection between the personal and professional aspects of teaching. *Teaching and Teacher Education*, 25(2): 297–308

This case study presents an interesting conceptualisation of teacher presence through the experience of an early career teacher in training.

4

WHY DO PRIMARY TEACHERS NEED TO HAVE HIGH STANDARDS OF PROFESSIONAL BEHAVIOUR?

DEBORAH WILKINSON

KEY WORDS: CODE OF CONDUCT; GROWTH MINDSET; HONESTY; INTEGRITY; REFLECTIVE PRACTICE; RESILIENCE; ROLE MODEL

INTRODUCTION

Why is it important for primary teachers to demonstrate high standards of professional behaviour, such as integrity, honesty, attendance, punctuality, resilience, subject knowledge and reflective practice? This chapter aims to explore these professional behaviours and how they link to the preamble of the Teachers' Standards and a school's conduct policy. Throughout this chapter you will be encouraged to reflect upon your professional behaviour and to link theory and practice together.

WHAT ARE PROFESSIONAL BEHAVIOURS AND WHY DO THEY MATTER?

The Organisation for Economic Co-operation and Development (OECD) (2018) asserts that teachers play a vital role in equipping pupils with the skills and knowledge required for success in an increasingly global, digital and complex world. To achieve this aim teachers need to build strong links with communities, build social responsibility and problem-solving skills and use effective pedagogies that foster student learning and nurture social and emotional skills. As an early career teacher your perceptions of teaching and its role in society will shape how you view your role, your professional behaviour and how you choose to teach children.

There are minimum requirements for teacher practice and conduct set by the Department for Education (2011) and it is worth considering the preamble of the Teachers' Standards as this outlines the professional practice, values and conduct expected of teachers:

> Teachers make the education of their pupils their first concern, and are accountable for achieving the highest possible standards in work and conduct. Teachers act with honesty and integrity; have a strong subject knowledge, (sic) keep their knowledge and skills as teachers up-to-date and are self-critical; forge positive professional relationships; and work with parents in the best interests of their pupils.

(DfE, 2011: 10)

This chapter explores key words from the preamble as important components of primary teachers' professional behaviour. Further discussion of professional relationships is explored in Chapter 5.

WHY DOES IT MATTER THAT I ACT WITH INTEGRITY AND HONESTY?

Teaching is a profession that is endowed with trust and high standards of behaviour and morals. Integrity is defined as following your morals or ethical convictions and 'doing the right thing'. Moral judgements are demonstrated through caring about others, showing empathy and respecting the rights of others. Danielson (2007) identifies honesty as the hallmark of integrity and asserts that teachers should be counted on for keeping their word and upholding confidentiality. A teacher's influence extends beyond the curriculum and the enduring impact is often to be found in the 'hidden curriculum' and the way in which teachers model behaviours. Teachers who expect students to display integrity must display integrity in their interactions with pupils (MacIntosh, 2014). Therefore, consider how you manage relationships.

- Do you behave fairly and consistently?

- If you expect children to listen to you, do you actively listen to them?

- How do you behave when children provide incorrect responses to questions?

- Do your classroom routines establish a climate whereby children feel safe to ask questions and know that mistakes are part of the learning process?

Developing a culture of trust and respect are the foundations for teaching and learning. Behaving with integrity goes some way to building that trust with children.

When in school, you should be inducted to the safeguarding procedures and know what your responsibilities are. You also need to know yourself – do you have strongly held beliefs with regards to politics or religion and how can you be certain that you are not undermining the rights of others. As an early career teacher you should demonstrate respect for a range of spiritual and cultural values, as well as diversity, social justice, freedom, democracy and the environment. This will be achieved through trusting relationships and showing fairness and openness.

WHY SHOULD TEACHERS' BEHAVIOUR BE IN LINE WITH THEIR SCHOOL CONDUCT POLICY?

When in school, all members of staff are expected to adhere to professional behaviours as outlined in the school's conduct policy. This policy should be shared with you as part of your induction to the school. A school conduct policy provides guidance on the standards of behaviour *all* school staff are expected to observe and is often closely aligned to the culture and ethos of the school. Teachers have a duty to keep pupils safe, to promote their welfare and to protect them from radicalisation, abuse (sexual, physical and emotional), neglect and safeguarding concerns. This duty is, in part, exercised through the development of respectful, caring and professional behaviours. Therefore, as an early career teacher you must have the highest standards of personal integrity as you are in a unique position to model behaviour to *all* pupils within the school. Professional behaviour also extends to your attendance, punctuality and how you organise yourself and your classroom. For example, if your classroom is untidy and disorganised, how can you expect children to find resources and to show independence? If you are going to be absent from school, it is important that you contact the school as soon as possible so that your lessons can be covered. You should also be punctual for school so that you are prepared for the day.

CASE STUDY WHY DO I NEED TO BE PREPARED FOR TEACHING?

Mrs James is an early career teacher in a three-form entry school. She has been struggling with workload and ensuring that she has sufficient subject knowledge to teach and plan sequences of lessons for the Year 3 team. The year group leader has asked her to submit her planning each Friday so that the teaching team are prepared for the upcoming week but Mrs James frequently misses these deadlines. Often the lesson plans are overdetailed and contain lots of activities that do not align closely to the learning objective of the lesson. As a result, tasks and the resources that are needed to support learning are poor or absent and other teachers in the team are frustrated. In addition to this, children are not being challenged at the appropriate level and due to the number of planned tasks do not have sufficient time to practise skills and consolidate skills and knowledge.

From whom could Mrs James seek advice to ensure that she is better supported?

According to Roeser et al. (2012), teaching is emotionally demanding and early career teachers need to acknowledge these feelings as they can result in 'burn-out' and mental health issues. The school community is well positioned to provide support; it is important to share your feelings with a member of the senior leadership team so that support can be provided. It is also worth remembering that as an early career teacher you have much to contribute and experienced teachers are keen to know your thinking. However, when working as part of a team, you need to ensure that planning is shared in a timely way so that others can be prepared for lessons.

Within a school environment, you will work with a range of people including teaching assistants, governors, cleaners, the caretaker, mid-day meals supervisors and office staff. As an early career teacher you must take care of yourself, others and the school property, so ensure that you are conversant with the health and safety rules that apply in your school. For example, if you are a smoker you will not be permitted to smoke on the school premises so you need to think carefully about where you will go should you need to have a cigarette during the school day. Ideally, this should be out of view of pupils.

On occasion, there may be a colleague or parent whom you do not 'like' or who may challenge your ideas. However, as a professional, you need to be supportive, courteous and affirmative to facilitate an unprejudiced dialogue with them. Remember that behaviour can be contagious so model the behaviours you would like to be on the receiving end of!

Staff meetings are a time for staff to work together to review policies for continuing professional development and to communicate important messages consistently to all members of staff. There may be a few people with 'strong personalities' who dominate the meeting but it is important that you try to contribute to discussions. Listen to the views of colleagues and treat their viewpoints respectfully. Try to be on time for the meeting and put your mobile phone on silent. You should not be scrolling through your phone during a meeting. Your phone should also stay in your bag when you are teaching your class; you can check for messages, etc. during breaktime!

The saying 'first impressions count' rings true in teaching. People will begin to form an opinion of you when you first contact the school to arrange a preliminary visit. Whether you send an email or phone the school, ensure that you communicate in a professional manner (this will include checking your emails to ensure that there are no grammatical or spelling errors). Dress in a professional way when you visit. Although the way in which a person dresses is a matter of personal choice, self-expression and/or linked to their religious and cultural customs, you must maintain an appropriate standard of dress (and personal appearance) which promotes a positive and professional image of the teaching profession. Your clothing and footwear should be safe and clean and take account of health and safety considerations for the phase that you are teaching. Your clothing should not be offensive or be too revealing (you should not be able to see through it, up it or down it!), should be free of any political or otherwise contentious slogans and not considered to be discriminatory. Some schools expect employees to wear identification badges at all times to assist pupils and visitors to the school. If this is the case, you need to ensure that you follow this directive.

CRITICAL QUESTION

Can I accept gifts?

There are occasions when pupils or parents/carers wish to pass small tokens of appreciation to you – for example, at Christmas or as a thank you – and this is acceptable. There is no national code of conduct or legislation about whether teachers are permitted to receive gifts from parents or pupils. However, the head teacher, governing body, local authority or academy trust may have a 'gift giving' policy and have rules about what is deemed as being acceptable. As an early career teacher act with integrity and take care that you do not accept any gift that might be construed by others as a bribe, or lead the giver to expect preferential treatment. It is unacceptable to receive gifts on a regular basis or of any significant value and you should not expect gifts from others as this is your job!

HOW DOES PROFESSIONAL BEHAVIOUR AFFECT CURRICULUM DELIVERY?

As an early career teacher, you are accountable for the progress, attainment and outcomes of children in your class. The preamble of the Teachers' Standards states that you should use your skills and knowledge to work in the best interests of your pupils, so at the end of the day consider how your lessons were received, what went well and why. How did you engage children in the lesson? How was the lesson adapted to meet the needs of all learners, did you have sufficient subject knowledge to ask probing questions and to challenge misconceptions or model key ideas? Have you created a safe learning environment whereby children can make mistakes and ask questions? How did you manage the behaviour of learners? The well-being and learning of the children in your class is at the centre of your professional practice. You should have high expectations for all pupils, be committed to addressing underachievement and work to help pupils progress regardless of their background and personal circumstances. In order to meet the needs of children, you need to know about their interests and backgrounds and weave these interests into your lessons.

CRITICAL QUESTION

Why is it important to know the subject content?

Knowing your subject matter is also fundamental. If you have a good understanding of the concepts that you are going to teach then you will feel more confident and may take risks with your teaching and plan more creative lessons (Wilkinson, 2016). Therefore, professional teachers take time to research the subject areas to be taught. To plan lessons that support learning, you should be aware of the subject-specific pedagogy for each subject area, key vocabulary and how the lessons form a sequence of learning.

THEORY FOCUS EFFECTIVE TEACHING

Shulman and Shulman (2007) probed the complexities of teaching and identified six domains of knowledge required for effective teaching as shown below:

Knowledge domain

1. Knowledge of learners - links to child development theories.

2. Knowledge of school contexts and the classroom dynamics and wider school community.

3. Knowledge of educational ends, values, philosophy of teaching.

4. Content knowledge - including the teacher's awareness of the value of group work, use of analogies and identification of misconceptions.

5. Curriculum knowledge - understanding of subject matter.

6. Classroom assessment.

In terms of subject-specific knowledge, teachers need to understand the content of what needs to be taught because having a good comprehension of the subject matter is important, according to Shulman (1986), as it will influence pedagogical content knowledge. The pedagogical content aspect of teaching requires teachers to know how to present the knowledge so that is can be

(Continued)

(Continued)

comprehended by learners. There is no one right way of presenting information to children so the teacher needs to make judgements and consider which approach (e.g. demonstration, analogy, illustration, explanation, example, etc.) is best matched to the child's needs. To achieve this, the teacher needs to consider the starting point of the child along with any preconceptions and misconceptions that they may have. The curricular knowledge refers to knowing how ideas fit together in a curriculum (e.g. understanding the requirements of the National Curriculum and planning for progression and sequencing of learning).

It is clear that teaching in primary school is reliant on a range of inter-related variables and socio-cultural factors such as educational biographies of teachers, as well as cultural perspectives within school settings (Danielson and Warwick, 2014). There needs to be an acknowledgement that personal, social and external influences affect teachers' choices when planning and delivering lessons. Teachers are also members of a school community and this also influences beliefs and practices. School communities are subjected to external pressures and reforms and this impacts upon priorities for schools and, consequently, teaching.

CASE STUDY HOW DO I DESIGN A CURRICULUM LINKED TO MY PERSONAL PHILOSOPHY OF 'GOOD PRACTICE'?

When on teaching placement, Mr Everett enjoyed using the outdoor learning environment to teach parts of the National Curriculum. However, when teaching in a school he noticed that none of his colleagues took children outside; because he was an early career teacher he did not wish to be 'different' so remained in the classroom.

How can you be confident in your teaching choices?

Mr Everett understood the theory relating to the value of outdoor learning, but was not confident to apply this to his teaching. As an early career teacher, you should make pedagogical decisions based upon research and evidence so that children can make good progress.

Effective teaching can impact in a positive, enriching way. Indeed, Hayes (2012) argues that education can be transformative if teachers treat pupils fairly and with respect; take their knowledge, views, opinions and feelings seriously; and value diversity and individuality. Consequently, as an early career teacher, you should present positive images of self-worth and belonging and think carefully about the role models you would like to refer to in your lessons. It is important that you build cultural capital in your lessons so that they may have a long-term positive effect on pupils' life chances. For example, do you encourage a diverse range of visitors into the classroom so that children can aspire to varied careers?

CRITICAL QUESTION

Why is it important that primary teachers know how to decolonise the curriculum?

Hayes (2012) asserts that children are not born with a view of themselves and their worth but that it is gradually shaped through their experiences. Therefore, as an early career teacher, you should aim to inspire pupils, by modelling enthusiasm for learning, a spirit of enquiry, honesty, tolerance, social responsibility, patience and a genuine concern for other people and their backgrounds. The Professional Behaviours section of the Core Content Framework and Early Career Framework for teachers in England, states that teachers should contribute *positively to the wider school culture and developing a feeling of shared responsibility for improving the lives of all pupils within the school* (DfE, 2019c: 24). Consider the behaviours that you will need to demonstrate when working through the following classroom link.

CLASSROOM LINKS HOW CAN I BE A CULTURALLY RESPONSIVE TEACHER?

To be a culturally responsive teacher you should avoid a 'colour-blind' approach; failure to acknowledge race and ethnicity results in some pupils feeling inferior and others superior. Patel (2019) argues that schools need to decolonise the curriculum and asserts that teachers need to deconstruct the knowledge that is taught in schools and to question what we accept as 'knowledge'. Therefore, as early career teachers, challenge the 'white, British and European curriculum' so that pupils know the contribution of a diverse group of people to our society.

Look at the curriculum that you are due to teach for history and/or science. Who are the people that the National Curriculum identifies? Do you think they would inspire the children in your class? Are they from varied and diverse backgrounds, representing and respecting the community that you are serving? Which alternative famous people would you like to teach the children in your class about?

As an early career teacher, you will be responsible for curating and sharing knowledge with pupils. The choices you make will impact upon student outcomes, so take care to share the connectiveness of humanity and think about how knowledge is constructed. For example, make reference to scientists or mathematicians from Greece, India, the Middle East and Africa to provide a richer educational experience for all pupils. Decolonising the curriculum is a contemporary challenge for the teaching profession. There are educationalists arguing against the decolonisation approach in the pursuit of academic integrity. Like other professions, teachers are engaged in thinking through this contentious issue that is situated in social and historical traditions. In terms of behaviours, it is important for teachers to demonstrate that they can engage critically with the debates. This requires the ability to be able to read a range of sources, analyse them objectively and contribute to discussions in a professional manner without causing offence.

HOW DOES MY PROFESSIONAL BEHAVIOUR HELP WHEN DEALING WITH SENSITIVE ISSUES?

When teaching certain areas of the curriculum, such as relationships and sex education or reproduction in science, it is feasible that this may lead to unplanned discussions. How you respond to questions and comments requires careful judgement and if you are unsure of your answer it is important that you seek advice from the designated safeguarding lead so that you are acting in accordance with advice given under Part 1 of Keeping Children Safe in Education. Your behaviour as a professional is therefore of vital importance. As a role model to children, it is appropriate that you are not only able to discuss issues sensitively, but also that you are able to follow the procedures within school if there is a safeguarding issue.

Similarly, a child may develop an infatuation with an adult who works with them. This may manifest itself in a child developing an attachment, dependency or becoming attracted to an adult. This must be reported to the head teacher so that action can be taken to avoid any hurt, distress or embarrassment. It is important that adults should be careful to ensure that no encouragement of any kind is given to the pupil. Again, the professional behaviour of the teacher is paramount and it is vital that an early career teacher understands professional boundaries.

There are occasions when staff in school settings need to have physical contact with pupils. However, it is crucial that this contact is appropriate to their professional role and in relation to the pupil's individual needs (and any agreed care plan). When physical contact is made with pupils this should be in response to their needs at the time, of limited duration and appropriate given their age, stage of development, gender, ethnicity, culture and background. There will be occasions when a distressed pupil needs comfort and reassurance and this may result in age-appropriate physical contact. As an early career teacher it is important that you are self-aware and that your contact is not threatening, intrusive or subject to misinterpretation. It is good practice to inform a colleague of when and how you offered comfort to a distressed pupil.

When teaching PE there may be occasions when you need to initiate physical contact with pupils in order to support a pupil so they can perform a task safely. This contact should be undertaken with the pupil's agreement and be for the minimum time necessary.

HOW ARE PROFESSIONAL BEHAVIOURS EXHIBITED BEYOND THE CLASSROOM?

Visits and clubs can enrich the curriculum but you should take particular care when supervising pupils in the less formal atmosphere of an educational visit, particularly in a residential setting, or after-school activity. As an early career teacher, you need to make sure that you are versed in the school's policy on educational visits and the health and safety policy.

CRITICAL QUESTION

Do I know how to access the school's risk assessment documentation?

Professional records should be stored appropriately. As a teacher, you should know how to access all documentation related to your role. You should also have your own clerical systems in place to ensure that you are able to access, store and handle documentation securely. Risk assessments for off-site visits must therefore be accessible. Whether you are the organiser of an off-site visit or an accompanying adult, it is essential that you have accessed the related risk assessment and had an opportunity to raise any concerns or questions.

When engaging on the educational visit professional behaviour is on show. When off-site, children and staff are representing their school. Members of the public will have a view on whether they perceive the children to be behaving in the way that is generally expected of primary-aged children. These perceptions help reinforce public trust in the teaching profession. Therefore, early career teachers need to ensure that they are comfortable to manage their children, even in less familiar surroundings.

WHY INCLUDE REFLECTION AS A PROFESSIONAL BEHAVIOUR?

Reflection plays an important role in professional life and, according to Pollard (2014), is necessary for acquiring expertise. The concept of reflective teaching is one that stems from the work of Dewey and is an orientation towards enquiry and the ability to think about experiences, to examine beliefs, practices and experiences in order to reach decisions. Dewey (1933) argued that professional learning is part of the experiential continuum and is a spiralling or cyclical process in which teachers monitor and evaluate and revise their practice. For the process to be successful, reflective teaching requires an attitude of open-mindedness; Dewey identified five characteristics or processes that an individual should pass through in order to deliver higher-quality standards of teaching (suggestion, problem-solving, generating a hypothesis, reasoning and testing).

THEORY FOCUS CONNECTING REFLECTIVE PRACTICE WITH PROFESSIONAL BEHAVIOUR

Schon expanded upon the work of Dewey and depicted reflective practice as a *dialogue of thinking and doing through which I become more skilful* (1987: 31). He introduced the concepts of reflection-in-action and reflection-on-action. Reflection-in-action is the process of shaping what is happening while working – for example, a teacher makes decisions about the suitability of their teaching during a lesson and considers which questions to ask or which task to set as the lesson progresses. If something is not working then reflection occurs and a conscious decision is made regarding what needs to happen next in the lesson. Reflection-on-action, however, happens after the activity or lesson when the teacher has the opportunity to judge how successful the lesson was and whether or not a change to the task would have resulted in different outcomes for learners.

Reflection is most effective when it is a social process in which the sharing of ideas with others is central to the development of a critical, open perspective of events (Wilkinson, 2016). It is common practice to have your lessons observed and your planning scrutinised; therefore, be open to suggestions and communicate in a positive manner. Schon highlights that the role of a more knowledgeable other is to *emphasize indeterminate zones of practice* (1987: 40) rather than to simply observe and point out errors or correct procedures. Here the focus is upon engaging you in a professional dialogue that seeks to analyse your classroom practice and to promote reflective thinking (Wilkinson, 2016). Reflecting upon the feedback that you are given and monitoring your progress with reference to advice given to you is a key way in which you will improve your teaching.

In addition to reflecting on your practice, take the opportunity to observe expert teachers. Ideally, ask if you can observe alongside an experienced teacher as they will notice things that you may have missed. They are able to explain why decisions may have been made, how complex material is broken into smaller steps or how to ensure that children are attentive so that they can learn new ideas. To get the most from observations, think carefully about the focus. It is also important to ask questions so that you can develop your practice. As an early career teacher, you are not expected to know everything and your mentor in school will expect you to ask lots of questions!

THEORY FOCUS WHY IS A GROWTH MINDSET SO IMPORTANT FOR TEACHERS?

Chappell (2003) argues that the best teachers are those who are never fully satisfied with their performance and see themselves to be lifelong learners. Indeed, you can learn a lot when a lesson does not go as planned and are able to adapt appropriately and learn from the experience. You need to remember that it is not possible to get everything right straight away and that you 'grow your understanding' step by step by considering what you will try next. Dweck (2015) maintains that intelligence in malleable and is not fixed. She identifies that a mindset is a set of abilities, attitudes and beliefs that people have about learning. Consequently, your belief about yourself as a learner will impact on how you learn from experiences. Are you someone who is prepared to accept challenges? Are you resilient to overcome problems or do you employ a 'fixed mindset reaction' whereby you become anxious, feel incompetent, deflated, look for excuses, become defensive or angry? If you get these feelings accept them – then remember that our abilities are developed and improved with practice and that we need to modify how we think about challenges. For example, you may say to yourself *I tried 'x' but it didn't work so now I will try 'y'*. Talking with colleagues can help you to review your practice and help you with new ideas. It is also important to think about the neuroplasticity of the brain. The brain can form new connections in response to an experience and, according to Dweck, *you can get smarter by rewiring your brain through practice* (2015: 18).

CHAPTER SUMMARY

To support your developing professional identity, this chapter has considered:

- why early career teachers need to be role models for professional behaviour;

- the importance of frameworks such as a code of conduct in school;

- the importance of seeking advice and support, particularly when seeking advice and help for sensitive issues;

- the importance of demonstrating professional behaviours beyond the primary classroom.

ASSIGNMENT LINKS

Occasionally, academic malpractice can occur in assignments. This may be intentional or unintentional, but is often a result of carelessness or work being completed in a rush. However, an academic malpractice says a lot about the individual's professional behaviour. It shows a lack of integrity. When producing assignments, take care to check that they have been completed as expected and that the correct procedures and conventions have been followed. Take time to proof-read written work or prepare adequately for oral presentations.

FURTHER READING

To develop your understanding of reflective practice, it is worth sourcing Schon's work in full.

Schon, D. (1987) *Educating the Reflective Practitioner.* San Francisco: Jossey-Bass

This article provides useful examples of how you can reflect on your teaching in order to secure the best outcomes for your pupils.

5

WHY ARE PROFESSIONAL RELATIONSHIPS IMPORTANT FOR PRIMARY TEACHERS?

GARY PARKES

KEY WORDS: COLLABORATION; EMOTIONAL INTELLIGENCE; RELATIONSHIPS; TRUST; TEACHER EFFECTIVENESS

INTRODUCTION

Why is it important for primary teachers to develop and maintain professional relationships in school and beyond? In order to discuss this question, we must consider how the relationships that teachers form underpin their capacity to be effective in their role. This chapter will give readers the opportunity to reflect upon their own values in terms of relationship building, and it will discuss the key role of effective professional relationships that enable effective teaching and learning, along with holistic child development. It will also consider the purpose of the professional relationships between: teachers and colleagues (both other teachers and colleagues from other agencies); teachers and parents/carers; and teachers and children.

THEORY FOCUS THE UNICEF CONVENTION ON THE RIGHTS OF A CHILD

The Convention on the Rights of the Child is the most rapidly ratified human rights treaty in history. More countries have ratified the Convention than any other human rights treaty in history – 196 countries have become State Parties to the Convention as of October 2015. The United Kingdom is one of these. Taken as a framework through which to view professional relationships in education, the UN Convention on the Rights of a Child underpins much of the thinking and discussion in this chapter. The following aspects of articles from the Convention have particular relevance and are referred to throughout:

> **3** 1. In all actions concerning children, whether undertaken by public or private social welfare institutions, courts of law, administrative authorities or legislative bodies, the best interests of the child shall be a primary consideration. ...

19 States Parties shall take all appropriate legislative, administrative, social and educational measures to protect the child from all forms of physical or mental violence, injury or abuse, neglect or negligent treatment, maltreatment or exploitation, including sexual abuse, while in the care of parent(s), legal guardian(s) or any other person who has the care of the child. ...

25 States Parties recognise the right of a child who has been placed by the competent authorities for the purposes of care, protection or treatment of his or her physical or mental health, to a periodic review of the treatment provided to the child and all other circumstances relevant to his or her placement. ...

29 States Parties agree that the education of the child shall be directed to: (a) The development of the child's personality, talents and mental and physical abilities to their fullest potential.

HOW DO PROFESSIONAL RELATIONSHIPS CONTRIBUTE TO TEACHER EFFECTIVENESS?

For the purposes of this chapter, three specific areas will be used in order to define what is meant by effectiveness: enabling learning; supporting holistic child development; and safeguarding. These areas can be considered as consistent goals of all of the many and varied activities of a teacher and, therefore, success in these three areas will be taken as a model to demonstrate effectiveness in the role (Articles 19 and 29 of the Convention on the Rights of a Child).

Initially, early career teachers might not see the explicit links between successful professional relationships and teacher effectiveness. Instead, effectiveness might be seen as personal competence demonstrated by a series of tasks to be achieved or ticked off and, as such, can be done independently – in some cases, even competitively. However, it is worth remembering that the levels of success each unique child experiences with academic learning, holistic development and safeguarding during their time in a school are never the sole responsibility of a single individual. Instead, success is supported by a community that interacts with the child and each other. The most effective teachers, therefore, are well-connected members of this community who make a proactive contribution to a larger team around each child.

CRITICAL QUESTION

How do professional relationships underpin a teacher's capacity to be effective?

To some, the completion of a task in order to prove competence is an adequate measure of effectiveness. However, this can encourage a performative approach to teaching because of the implication that the completion of tasks that demonstrate technical competence, such as creating planning documents or achieving test result targets, is an achievement in itself rather than considering the value of these activities to the child throughout their time in school. In addition, while this task-focused view is still seen to value and promote professional behaviours in teachers, it is done in a way that makes teacher professionalism an extra or other to the required standards and competencies.

An opposing viewpoint would put the teacher's professional behaviour first and at the centre of all of their activities. This alternative view sees the teacher's professional identity and their contribution to the larger community through the relationships they form as an absolutely necessary underpinning needed in order for teachers to be effective. Using professional behaviours and relationships as the foundation for teachers' activities, technical competence can be enhanced through collaborative engagement with a critical community that taps into a range of views and expertise, making the measurable tasks both more purposeful and meaningful. These professional attributes also play a key role in the safeguarding of children, where trust and positive relationships are vital to the honest sharing of information and confidentiality.

Having established an argument for the need to be a purposeful and useful part of a larger community, teachers should consider how they can best contribute to it and learn from it. As with all groups and communities, communication between its members is a key factor to cohesion, productivity and success. The quality, clarity, honesty and degree of collaboration in this communication is largely dependent on the quality of relationships formed within it.

CLASSROOM LINK MEMBERS OF A COMMUNITY

Choose one of the following areas: teaching and learning, safeguarding, holistic child development. First, list all of the members in and around the school community that an effective teacher would successfully form a professional relationship with. Then, linking to ideas about teacher identity from Chapters 1 and 2 of this book, recognise and note which aspects of your professional identity might support effective professional relationships. Are there any other aspects that you could add to help with this?

WHY IS IT IMPORTANT TO FORM RELATIONSHIPS WITH COLLEAGUES?

CRITICAL QUESTION

Why don't all teachers collaborate?

A factor sometimes cited as a reason for working independently is a lack of trust. Collaboration by its nature requires participants to allow themselves to be exposed to a certain level of vulnerability. This is because true collaboration involves shared judgement and decision-making and with this comes the potential to negatively impact the emotions and esteem of the individuals involved. Some teachers may also place great value on the importance of recognition and fear that this may be diluted or lost completely if they share their ideas with others. In the worst case, teachers fear, 'carrying' less effective colleagues and suffering increased workload as a result while other team members are perceived to benefit from very little effort. While this should not be dismissed, whether teachers feel valued and recognised for their contributions can be and should be addressed by the leadership of the school and the resulting working culture. If this is not in place, collaboration may be harder to establish but, even so, proactive members of a collaborative group can create their own positive work culture that appropriately recognises and values the contributions of its members even if this is not the prevailing culture overall.

Another common reason given for not working collaboratively in teaching is the perceived loss of autonomy. Teachers question if their own values, standards and systems may be compromised if they are not in full charge of decision-making. This can lead to teachers becoming overly protective of their work and the closing down of open and honest sharing. In this scenario teachers compete to be the most effective as individuals, each having a standpoint where they consider that their own learnt experiences have taken them to a position where they 'know best'. This can be problematic not least because it involves subjective and often unilateral judgement of both their own knowledge and skills and those of their colleagues.

A perceived loss of autonomy and a lack of trust can act as very real barriers to collaboration. This can also link to the previously mentioned view that some teachers may have about effectiveness being something that individuals can demonstrate by completing tasks requiring technical proficiency. However, a reoccurring theme of this chapter is that teacher effectiveness cannot be truly observed unless the impact of such tasks is seen to contribute to the levels of success experienced by individual pupils. In essence, in order for a teacher to be judged as effective, their contribution needs to be seen and felt by the members of the school community in the inter-connected reality of everyday, rather than as an idea or statement of an individual. To overcome these perceived barriers, an understanding of this type of professional relationship is needed and also the skills required to support it.

CRITICAL QUESTION

What is the purpose of my relationship with colleagues in school?

Teachers cite professional development, reduced workload and an improved focus on children as some of the benefits of collaboration with colleagues (Muckenthaler et al., 2020). It allows members of the group to contribute their own expert input of ideas and proposals and also hear a range of other expert views on a similar subject. This leads to ideas being scrutinised, refined and improved. As well as the valuable feedback and analysis of these ideas, group members can often benefit from raised levels of motivation as proposals evolve and improve at a speed and level of consideration that is not possible when working alone. At the centre of this lays the desire to change and improve practice for the benefit of the children in the school.

WHY IS IT IMPORTANT TO ESTABLISH A COLLABORATIVE WORK CULTURE?

We will look at the two main ways of organising collaborative groups. In the first model, full collaboration is used to gain the views, experiences, varied skills and knowledge of its members until a point is reached where a decision or judgement needs to be made. If consensus cannot be reached then the final decision-maker uses their position to analyse all of the input and decide the direction forward. This kind of working group is more effective when the project that the group is working on will have a wide impact upon the working practices of a significant number of people and will therefore affect systematic school-wide change. The second model, perhaps more commonly and informally used, takes contributions from a group in which each of its members have equal status and say. This model, used for a wide range of project types and perhaps at a smaller scale, can prove to be more problematic if trust is not first established; this can lead to members attempting to avoid feeling vulnerable and possibly being reluctant to contribute or take risks which can have a negative impact on positive development and change in practice.

Feeling safe and taking risks are often key levers for development and improvement. A lack of trust can be enough to prevent this from happening. The trust in question here is that between colleagues. Without it, the benefits of true collaboration may be lost and intended positive change and improvements to practice lost with it. Teachers must feel comfortable in order to suggest and try new things.

Relational trust is created though the continued practice of trusting and being trusted by colleagues. This has the effect of making the trust active and current rather than historical. Being explicit about this practice may help to make that trust more visible and therefore grow in strength and value. The strategy of showing trust towards colleagues over a period of time will show that you have an active level of trust in them that is current and relevant (Cranston, 2011). Another strategy is to allow yourself to be vulnerable to judgement or criticism. This explicitly shows the trust you put in your collaborators but also the way you react if challenged can play a part in forming a more professional collaborative relationship. For example, if, after some criticism, you show that you are not offended or upset by the challenge and accept it as valid comment and respond with a professionally focused question or comment, this sets a 'norm' for if this were to happen again in the future. This may encourage colleagues to lower their guard, as they become more likely over time to trust that criticism will not lead to conflict and is not personal. This begins to establish accepted working norms where constructive criticism is focused on ideas, plans and decisions rather than the people that contributed them. This helps all participants to feel safe and focus upon the professional aspects of any conversation.

CLASSROOM LINK ESTABLISHING TRUST

Think of real examples of when you will have the opportunity to establish trust when working with colleagues. Make a list of these. Include staff meetings or INSET days but don't forget the less formal settings as well, like car sharing or playground duty. For each instance list specific examples of how you might establish trust with the colleagues involved. For example: on playground duty, respond to criticism of some year group planning positively by acknowledging the colleague's view and making a suggestion or asking a question.

Skills and attributes that are helpful when beginning to work with collaborative groups and establishing trust include:

- explicitly showing the trust of others in the group;

- a focus on improvement in practice for the benefit of children (not people in the group);

- contributing expert knowledge;

- humility (your way may not be the right way);

- genuinely listening to others;

- offering constructive, project-focused, solution-based feedback;

- a willingness to take risks (make yourself vulnerable because an idea might not work);

- visible recognition of the contributions of others;

- being emotionally resilient if your contributions are criticised (don't take it personally).

WHY FORM RELATIONSHIPS WITH COLLEAGUES FROM OTHER AGENCIES?

Another type of collegiate relationship that teachers can form is with other professionals that are not school-based but nonetheless form an important part of the community around the child. This is similar to but distinct from the professional relationships teachers form with other adults in school. Professional colleagues might include social workers, healthcare workers or the police, for example. It can sometimes become necessary to be involved in the more holistic basic needs of a child, such as if a safeguarding concern has been raised or if a child living in care (looked after) joins your class (Article 25 of the Convention on the Rights of a Child). In these instances, the team around the child can offer multi-agency expertise and a holistic picture of any issues surrounding the child, as well as expert insight into specific aspects.

CRITICAL QUESTION

What is the purpose of the relationships with professionals from other agencies?

The purpose of the professional collaborative relationship in this case is to contribute as an expert in the specific area of schooling, but also to gather additional information from the wider group that may have an impact on the child in school. As such, the skills and attributes that will have the most positive effect in instances like these include being:

- knowledgeable (prepare and do your research);

- compassionate but not over emotional;

- honest and trustworthy;

- understanding;

- a concise and effective communicator;

- able to prioritise and record useful information.

These types of collegiate professional relationships should be central to your professional development and your effectiveness as a teacher. Not only will they prevent teachers from relying on dated knowledge and making unilateral decisions based on these, they can also improve motivation, reduce workload and be a real lever for change and improvement. As a result, the practice and provision surrounding the children in the school will consistently improve. However, the relationships formed with teachers and other professionals are not the only ones that produce benefits for children.

RELATIONSHIPS WITH CARERS, PARENTS AND FAMILIES

A successful professional relationship between a teacher and the parent/carer of a child leads to useful, productive and rewarding outcomes for the child and all the adults involved, but it is also potentially the most complex and, in some circumstances, can be the source of some tension. Earlier we looked at the professional relationships teachers form between themselves and colleagues. The relationships that teachers form with parent/carers, while still described as professional, are distinctly different for a number of reasons.

Traditionally, the younger year groups – especially the Early Years Foundation Stage – have capitalised on establishing strong links with home. However, the benefits of positive relationships between teacher and parent/carer in all phases of education are also well documented. Some studies report that parental involvement in a child's schooling has a powerful impact on behaviour and overall pupil outcomes (Davidson and Case, 2018; Santiago et al., 2016). This is another example of teacher effectiveness being demonstrated by a positive impact on pupils – as a direct result of successful professional relationships and the productive collaboration that this enables.

While the argument for the benefits of parental involvement, cooperation and collaboration are strong, it is important that teachers understand the nature of this type of relationship and why it might lead to tensions if not handled properly. A very important and distinct difference between the relationships set up between colleagues and the relationships between teachers and parents or carers is that there are no professional expectations placed upon the role of the parent/carer. Where the teacher should and is expected to behave in a 'professional' manner, the parent may communicate in any way they deem appropriate. This can range from being very friendly and sociable to aggressive and threatening behaviour. While the latter is thankfully rare, it is worth trying to understand why this sometimes happens and considering strategies to build successful positive relationships in an attempt to reap the widespread benefits that these can bring.

CRITICAL QUESTION

Why might there be tensions in my relationships with parents?

If we consider the imbalance and complexities of this type of relationship we might begin to unpick where some of the potential tensions might arise. When a parent or carer is in conversation with a teacher, they come with a subjective view of what school should be and what the job of a teacher is. This view will have been formed by their own experiences of school, by their friends and family, by other parents (some of whom they will disagree with), by the media and by their own child. This spectrum of views can be broadened further still when considering the varied religious and cultural backgrounds of each family. The teacher comes to the conversation as a trained, qualified professional with an understanding of child development, knowledge of the National Curriculum, school values and national developments in education. There is also an imbalance in the power dynamic too in that the parent/carer has the overriding say in what they see as best for the child (unless there are safeguarding concerns). This imbalance of starting points may be further added to when considering the complexities of the purpose of this relationship.

First and foremost, the relationship should benefit the child. This two-way communication will both support the parent/carer's understanding of the school and the school's assessment of the child's development and potential needs and support the teacher in understanding the unique child in the context of their family and home life. This sharing of information can be used to support the child's development in both the home and school environments. This relationship can also help to strengthen the professional teacher–child relationship discussed later in this chapter.

Below are a few examples of the type of information that may be useful to teachers in order for them to form a stronger relationship with the parent/carer and their child and support them better in school:

- home routines, bedtimes, how the child spends their time;

- the behavioural expectations of parent/carers;

- languages spoken at home;

- cultural expectations or restrictions;

- medical issues and or educational needs;

- bereavements and changes to the family circumstances.

Information from the teacher that can help the parent/carer support the child with their development at home might include:

- summative and formative assessment of the child's development;

- the child's behaviour in relation to the school's expectations and other children;

- specific targets/learning/activities to support child development at home;

- information about school values and aims;

- in some circumstances, resources might be provided to help children at home.

The sharing of this information in this two-way relationship can be enormously productive with obvious benefits for the child. Another consequence of a successful teacher–parent/carer relationship is that of consistency between home and school. Consistency in behavioural expectations and work ethic gives children less opportunity to question systems and decisions at school and at home as the same message is applied in both circumstances. This is also a very real opportunity to reach out to parent/carers and show them that the school is on their side and has the best interests of their child at heart.

One of the complexities to this relationship is that while the leadership of any school will cite the benefits and child-centred purpose of teacher–parent/carer relationships, they will also be aware of the outward-facing nature of the relationship and how each teacher is a representative of the school, its values and its effectiveness. Because of this, the teacher must be aware of this responsibility in all of their interactions with parent/carers and ensure their conduct can be judged to be professional.

The following list aims to help teachers consider the point of view of the parent/carer and is followed by suggestions to support the development of strong relationships with them while remaining professional.

Parent/carers:

- want to feel that teachers know their child;
- want to feel that the teacher's best interests lay with them and their child and that they can be trusted (Article 3 of the Convention on the Rights of a Child);
- want to be listened to and understood;
- want to feel that the teacher is compassionate and knowledgeable and will help and support them.

In order to support this, teachers should:

- be friendly and approachable;
- get to know each unique child;
- establish trust;
- where appropriate, find out as much information as possible prior to any communication/meeting;
- really listen and seek to understand;
- communicate concisely with clarity and empathy;
- be resilient to potential emotional displays;
- be proactive in seeking relationships with parent/carers.

As building these relationships is integral to the development of your effectiveness as a teacher, it should be considered a part of your overall workload. It is therefore important to consider how to systematise and build in opportunities for this in your regular working day which both protects your own time and proactively plans for time to establish and maintain relationships.

The relationships with the adults in the community around each child that we have discussed so far in this chapter all serve the purpose of refining the practice surrounding the development of children and, as a result, improving your effectiveness as a teacher. They are also a key contribution to making your professional relationships with children as supportive and successful as possible.

WHY IS IT IMPORTANT TO FORM EFFECTIVE RELATIONSHIPS WITH CHILDREN?

With great power there must also come – great responsibility!

(Lee, 1962: 11)

Even if you recognise this quote from the Spider-Man stories, you may be wondering why it is relevant in this section about relationships with children. As a student or newly qualified teacher, the relationships you form with the children in the school are the ones in which you have the most power. To underestimate the power dynamic in these relationships is a failure to recognise and understand the position the teacher holds in relation to the children.

In light of the significance of this, we will explore what professional relationships with children might look like and why it is necessary for them to be different from social relationships or even other professional relationships with colleagues or parents. Schools expect teachers to lead on children's learning and development; relationships with other children; and the behaviour expected of them. Also, as part of the power of this leadership, children expect the adult in the room to have the authority to maintain order and keep them safe. Because of this, the relationship between teacher and child cannot be an equal one as the child has considerably less power. Being aware of and managing this power so that it is used for the benefit of the child (Article 3 of the Convention on the Rights of a Child) is the professional responsibility of the teacher. Although it is not always the case, often when we choose to establish a social relationship it is formed through two-way contributions from both sides of an equal nature. As humans, we may even favour social relationships where we feel among equals rather than competing for power. This continues as a form of 'give and take' where reciprocity maintains the bond going forward. However, if teachers attempt to establish this type of 'social friendship' with children, the two-way nature of the social arrangement may quickly prove problematic. Unlike the social arrangements we make, the child in the (professional) relationship is under no obligation to reciprocate or offer the teacher anything in return. Unlike social relationships, where you may choose to walk away from a non-reciprocal friendship, teachers are professionally bound to their relationships with children and for this reason some may feel decidedly one-sided.

The social and emotional factors that drive our social relationships are not ones that are useful in determining effective professional relationships with children for the reasons explained above. It is important to remember, however, that even professional opinion around what constitutes an effective teacher–child relationship is complex and blurry. This is because we are discussing human beings and not synthetic mechanisms or computer algorithms where outputs are largely predictable based on what you input.

CASE STUDY

A new child joined your class a week ago. They seem to be finding it hard to settle in to the school and are reluctant to mix with other children. They choose to spend time alone during breaks and do not offer contributions to lessons unless asked by the teacher. Based on these few interactions, your initial assessment is that they are articulate and knowledgeable. The standard of work they present is above average apart from poor spelling and they have not displayed any disruptive behaviour. Other children have more pronounced needs and are demanding of your time.

What should your priorities be in order to establish a professional relationship with this child and help them to develop positive relationships with their peers?

How might your relationships with colleagues, the class and the child's parents support your actions?

Positive relationships also assist with teachers' safeguarding duties (Article 19 of the Convention on the Rights of a Child). The professional relationships you establish with children play a key role in the effectiveness of safeguarding procedures. Strong professional relationships where the teacher has a good knowledge of the child as an individual and where the child trusts the teacher can significantly enhance safeguarding provision. Having a good knowledge of the child as an individual, their home life and their general behaviour and demeanour will make it much easier to observe if something is different, such as:

- a reduced level of cleanliness and/or a lack of clean, laundered clothes;

- a change in temperament or mood swings;

- bruising or other marks on the body;

- a marked change in conversation subject matter or new inappropriate interests;

- a sudden lack of confidence or reluctance to participate.

This is not an exhaustive list but provides examples of things that are easier to notice if the teacher has a strong professional relationship by having a good knowledge of the child as an individual.

Noticing a change like this can then lead to steps detailed in your school's safeguarding policy to follow up any concerns.

Furthermore, if the child views the teacher as honest and trustworthy and feels that the teacher has their best interests at heart they are more likely to disclose information that may also lead to concerns about the child's welfare. One of the purposes of the relationship is to help the child feel that the teacher is both in a position of authority and can be trusted.

CRITICAL QUESTION

What do strong professional relationships with children look like?

We have established earlier in the chapter that teachers need to be aware of the power dynamic in their relationships. From the teacher's point of view this type of professional relationship is about giving and being a supportive provider without seeking reward or recognition from the child and this may feel one-sided and different to social relationships. It may be helpful to examine the functions required of the relationship in order to understand it further. For a child's needs to be appropriately met, an effective professional relationship might aim to:

- support the child to feel they are able to ask the teacher for help and advice and not feel anxious in doing so;

- support the child to feel safe because the teacher demonstrates the appropriate levels of organisation and authority when appropriate and that decisions the teacher makes are fair and consistent;

- support the child to feel that the teacher likes them and has an awareness of them as an individual;

- convey to the child that the teacher is honest and trustworthy and has the child's best interests at heart (Article 3 of the Convention on the Rights of a Child);

- support the child to feel that the teacher is knowledgeable and considerate.

While this is not an exhaustive list, these main aims can help us to develop an overall understanding of the complexity and purpose of the relationship. Each of these aspects supports the professional relationship in contributing to the development of learning; social, emotional and physical development; and safeguarding all children.

CLASSROOM LINKS RELATIONSHIPS WITH CHILDREN

Consider each bullet point above in turn and note two or three things per point that you can do in order to establish and strengthen that aspect of your relationships with children. For example, for

(Continued)

(Continued)

support the child to feel that the teacher likes them and has an awareness of them as an individual teachers may seek opportunities to ask them questions about their hobbies and interests. Once this is understood, a teacher may subsequently make comments about the child's hobbies and interests to show that they have remembered this and value the child. For *support the child to feel safe* the teacher could establish class rules with the children, agreeing what is fair and consistently being seen to hand out rewards and sanctions impartially and appropriately.

CHAPTER SUMMARY

Why are professional relationships important for primary teachers?

This chapter has shown how relationships underpin effective teaching, the well-being/safeguarding of children and collegiality within primary schools. Professionalism requires primary school teachers to communicate effectively and forge positive relationships with all stakeholders.

ASSIGNMENT LINKS

When producing assignments that relate to teaching and learning, behaviour management, or working with others, consider the importance of relationships. For example, if writing an essay about effective planning you may want to consider the purposes of professional relationships with children and the impact of this on your chosen pedagogy to bring out the best in your pupils.

FURTHER READING

Education Endowment Foundation (2021) Evidence summaries. Available at: https://educationen dowmentfoundation.org.uk/evidence-summaries/. Accessed 1 March 2021

The Education Endowment Foundation has a practical toolkit to show the effects of parental engagement, behaviour interventions with pupils and the deployment of teaching assistants. It is worth exploring the reports to help inform the importance of effective relationships with these stakeholders in primary education.

6

WHY ARE PROFESSIONAL NETWORKS AND RESEARCH NETWORKS USEFUL FOR PRIMARY TEACHERS?

KIRSTIE HEWETT

KEYWORDS: PROFESSIONAL DEVELOPMENT; PROFESSIONAL KNOWLEDGE; EVIDENCE AND RESEARCH ENGAGEMENT; AUTONOMY AND AGENCY; WELL-BEING

INTRODUCTION

Why build professional networks? This chapter sets out some key considerations for primary teachers to help them build effective networks to support their growth as professionals. It explores what networks have to offer and how they enable primary teachers to maintain and develop their professional identities. It goes on to look at the personal and professional benefits of networks, exploring why these matter and how they can support teachers to thrive. Different kinds of networks are considered and readers are invited to reflect on how they might go about building networks that matter to them. The list of networks referred to in this chapter is not by any means exhaustive. Other local and national networks are available and are likely to be well worth exploring.

WHAT IS A NETWORK?

A network can be defined as *a group or system of interconnected people … or a group of people who exchange information and contacts for professional or social purposes*. To network is to *interact with others to exchange information and develop professional or social contacts* (Lexico, 2021).

In the Early Career Framework networks are identified as part of *Professional Behaviours Standard 8 – Fulfil wider professional responsibilities*, specifying that one of the ways in which a teacher develops as a professional is through *strengthening pedagogical and subject knowledge by participating in wider networks* (DfE, 2019c: 24).

This enables a teacher to build essential skills and lay strong groundwork for meeting Standard 8, as they move on from the Early Career Framework to the Teachers' Standards, which *continue to define the level of practice at which all qualified teachers are expected to perform* (DfE, 2011: 6) and state specifically that a teacher must:

develop effective professional relationships with colleagues, knowing how and when to draw on advice and specialist support;

take responsibility for improving teaching through appropriate professional development, responding to advice and feedback from colleagues.

(2011: 13)

HOW DO NETWORKS SUPPORT TEACHERS' KNOWLEDGE?

In their review of the research which aims to uncover what makes great teaching, Coe at al. identify the importance of strong pedagogical and subject knowledge as the factor which is most robustly supported by evidence, concluding that *the most effective teachers have deep knowledge of the subjects they teach* (2015: 2). Guerriero also recognises teacher knowledge a key aspect of teacher professionalism, stating that teaching is:

a knowledge-rich profession with teachers as 'learning specialists.' As professionals in their field, teachers can be expected to process and evaluate new knowledge relevant for their core professional practice and to regularly update their knowledge base to improve their practice and to meet new teaching demand.

(2014: 3)

When analysing and responding to ongoing learning in the classroom, teachers draw on their specialist knowledge of the teaching and learning process to support them in making sound pedagogical decisions which contribute to the creation of effective teaching and learning environments (Guerriero, 2014).

Two kinds of knowledge, pedagogical and subject, are identified in the Early Career Framework. However, as mentioned in Chapter 4 of this book, there are multiple domains of subject knowledge. For example, in addition to pedagogical knowledge and subject knowledge, early career teachers may want to consider their curricula knowledge. This is the teacher's knowledge of the full curriculum studied by the learner, who is immersed in the learning of many different subjects and topics at a particular year group, at any point in time. This enables the teacher to make crucial links between aspects of a particular subject and other subjects that pupils may be learning. Shulman (1986) stresses that the teacher needs to be able to relate this curriculum knowledge to what has been taught in the same subject area previously and what comes next.

CRITICAL QUESTION

How can networks support teachers' subject knowledge?

All areas of a teacher's knowledge (including subject matter, ways in which this can most powerfully be transmitted to learners at different stages and knowledge of the whole curriculum) will be deepened through experience. Thus, building networks which allow new teachers to engage with a wealth of wide-ranging knowledge and understanding from fellow professionals supports the growth of all areas of knowledge that are essential for effective teaching.

Continuing to build knowledge throughout your training and as you begin your teaching career is therefore a crucial aspect of a teacher's professionalism. Knowledge is built through the process of professional development. Professional development has the potential to hold such value for teachers that much research has been conducted to discover the best models to support teachers to develop continuously in this way.

Effective professional development is defined by Bubb and Earley as:

> *an ongoing process encompassing all formal and informal learning experiences that enable staff in schools, individually and with others, to think about what they are doing, enhance their knowledge and skills and improve ways of working so that pupil learning and well-being are enhanced as a result. It should achieve a balance between individual, group, school and national needs; encourage a commitment to professional and personal growth; and increase resilience, self-confidence, job satisfaction and enthusiasm for working with children and colleagues.*
>
> (2007: 4, cited in Bubb and Earley, 2010: 2)

The authors assert that: *Staff development makes a crucial difference. It ultimately leads to school improvement whether couched in terms of better teaching and learning, or student and staff welfare and well-being* (Bubb and Earley, 2010: 3).

One way teachers might build their professional knowledge of specific curriculum areas is by becoming involved with subject associations. These are membership groups whose members have interest and sometimes expertise in a particular subject. They allow you to keep up to date and to be part of a community of teachers. They can be a really useful source of professional development through their publications and forums. Some may also run specific events which you might be able to attend. Subject organisations are independent of the government and publish interesting position statements or responses to government initiatives and world events. For example, when schooling was disrupted due to the COVID-19 pandemic in 2020–1 many subject associations made resources to support home-schooling available. The Council for Subject Associations maintains a free subject association directory in which you can find details of specific associations organised by subject. This can be accessed from their website: https://www.subjectassociations.org.uk/the-cfsa-directory/. Primary teachers will need to seek out content related to primary, as the subject associations encompass multiple key stages and phases of education.

CLASSROOM LINK REFLECTING ON YOUR PROFESSIONAL KNOWLEDGE

Create a grid listing subject areas that you may teach in the left-hand column (for example: light, the Great Fire of London, rivers). Now reflect on three kinds of knowledge that you need: subject knowledge, pedagogic knowledge and curricula knowledge. Create a column for each. Taking each kind of knowledge one at a time, consider how confident you feel about your knowledge of the subject itself; powerful ways in which you know you can share this knowledge with your pupils; and the extent to

(Continued)

(Continued)

which you know that you can make effective and meaningful links to cross-curricular and prior learning. Using a scale of 1–5 where 5 represents 'very confident, teaching outcomes are excellent' and 1 represents 'not very confident, teaching outcomes aren't yet secure', go through each subject or topic. Now identify one way in which you could use a network to increase your scaled score by 1 point. In the rest of the chapter, a range of different networks will be considered so you will be able to match some actions later if you're not yet sure of the best approach.

HOW DOES ENGAGEMENT WITH RESEARCH SUPPORT TEACHERS' PROFESSIONAL IDENTITIES?

The Early Career Framework highlights the importance of building and using networks in order to *learn how to develop as a professional by engaging critically with research and discussing evidence with colleagues* (DfE, 2019c: 24).

Picture a calm, orderly classroom where students are engaged, interested and motivated to complete their work. We may think of these factors as highly desirable characteristics of effective classrooms and yet, according to Coe (2013), they are not necessarily signs that effective learning is taking place. Of course, these traits are desirable because to be able to observe such features we would consider that the classroom is well managed, the pupils feel safe and show a strong work ethic. Such conditions are key to providing a classroom climate in which effective learning can occur. However, according to Coe (2013), these are not necessarily indicators of effective learning themselves. Teachers juggle many considerations every day – for example: what will be taught, how best to teach, how to adapt learning for learners with different starting points and needs, how to manage behaviour effectively, how to assess pupils' learning in a meaningful way and so on. So how do we look beyond superficial factors to ensure that truly effective learning is taking place in our classrooms? Wiliam (2018: 164) asserts *teachers can change their practice in many ways. Some will benefit students, and some will not, and this is where the research evidence is important.* The importance of using research evidence as a basis to support decision-making and to help us answer the key question of what truly effective learning looks like is a significant and increasingly prominent subject for discussion. It can be argued that the professional teacher needs to understand research-informed pedagogies and the signs that effective learning is taking place, in the same way that the professional doctor needs to understand research-based treatments and the signs that treatments are working.

CRITICAL QUESTION

What is evidence-based education?

Firth (2017) describes evidence-based education as:

> the idea that research of various kinds should be used to inform decisions about teaching and learning. It is conceived of as an alternative to teaching practice that is guided by intuition and/or experience.

Again, the Early Career Framework recognises the value of this approach, specifying that teachers should learn that *Reflective practice, supported by... learning from educational research, is ... likely to support improvement* (DfE, 2019c: 24).

Research networks aim to support the relationship between research and classroom practice, ensuring that the teaching profession is informed by the best evidence. Educational research offers an opportunity to reflect deeply on our practice, helping us to identify what effective practice is, what the key components of that effective practice are and why they matter, enabling us to engage in purposeful professional growth which supports our understanding of excellence in teaching.

Evidence-based practice supports teachers to solve problems that arise in the classroom: for example, how to support a particular group of pupils to make good progress through quality-first teaching or interventions. Weston and Clay (2018: 113) assert:

> Research evidence can help you understand what has worked, where, why and for whom. It can indicate what is plausibly useful to try and what is less plausibly useful. It can challenge 'common sense' and give us new insights, identify things that 'feel right' but may be less helpful and save precious time, effort and money in the process.

Therefore, engaging with the evidence base informed by research can empower the professional teacher, enhancing a sense of professional judgement and supporting teachers to develop their practice in effective ways. Firth (2018) highlights that it is crucial that development as professionals is enriched by the ever-growing wealth of knowledge and understanding underpinned by high-quality research. He also identifies the value of building networks which involve teachers from other institutions, enabling all to draw on a broader pool of knowledge. Critical engagement with and discussion of research in collaboration with professional colleagues allows us to reflect deeply on our own philosophy and practice. Seeing our classroom through the lens of another's perceptions of what makes a particular practice, resource or intervention effective can be valuable in helping us to use professional conversations to develop excellence in teaching. Teachers who are research literate have the capacity to secure stronger outcomes for learners in their care and BERA (2014) note that being research literate and providing opportunities for teachers to engage in the research process correlates closely with high-quality teaching and pupil outcomes.

THEORY FOCUS WHAT IS THE VALUE OF ENGAGING WITH RESEARCH AND EVIDENCE?

In their book *Unleashing Great Teaching*, Weston and Clay explore ways in which teachers can use research evidence to develop their classroom practice. They too highlight the importance of ensuring that expertise is credible:

(Continued)

(Continued)

when engaging in a professional learning process, teachers want to be sure that they're getting good advice. This means ensuring that professional learning is informed by a strong evidence base.

(Weston and Clay, 2018: 6)

They suggest that teachers consider carefully what they are looking for from engagement with research to help them to engage with meaning and purpose. It may be that teachers want to look for evidence to find why and how a particular practice is effective for learners, or perhaps they wish to find out whether a particular practice has a base in evidence at all. They may be looking to find out a particular context in which a practice has been judged to be effective for others, or seeking to understand a different perspective.

Weston and Clay (2018) also identify that engagement with the evidence base is not always carefree, noting that potential problems to consider include: filtering research and findings that confirm what we already think rather than seeking that which challenges our thinking; and ensuring the evidence base of anything we consider is sufficiently robust to hold validity. The authors suggest working with expert practitioners and facilitators to help to ensure quality. This expertise may be in the form of experienced teachers in local schools, links with local organisations or links with higher education institutions that can support teachers to make the most of their engagement with evidence.

Weston and Clay also emphasise the key role of networks in supporting the highly valuable practice of engaging with research and its potential impact on the profession of teaching:

every teacher needs to be able to draw upon the collective expertise of the whole profession, not just the ideas already in their head, not just the best ideas in their school. This is a simple, yet powerful idea. Every teacher in every school needs to be linked into national networks of knowledge. Every professional learning opportunity needs to tap into the best ideas out there, not just an idea that feels new or interesting within their school. This idea opens new avenues for teachers to become experts in more specialist areas and to use this expertise to have impact on more students.

(Weston and Clay, 2018: 3)

CLASSROOM LINK ENGAGING IN PROFESSIONAL CONVERSATIONS

Engaging in networks beyond your school offers space to reflect on classroom practice and its outcomes on pupil learning and development, *reaching beyond your own classroom to the wider world of ideas, research and professional development courses* (Frost et al., 2018: 155). This is not to say you will always agree with professional colleagues, but through professional debate we can get to the heart of principles that underpin effective pedagogy, helping us to build our understanding of how different children learn. Monbiot (2019) proposes that engaging in such bridging networks, which seek to bring together people with different backgrounds and perspectives to share their values, ideas and experiences, allows us to create *rich, engaging, inclusive and generous communities.*

A good place to start is to find out which networks your school is already involved in. For example, your school may belong to a locality network or cluster which involves all schools in the same area, or to an academy network which involves schools in the same multi-academy trust. Networks are then typically organised by role or focus - such as early career teachers, SEND leads, English leads or Year 6 teachers - so the perfect network may well be up and running, and therefore easy to join. If there aren't any existing groups already in operation, why not set up your own to enable teachers to discuss best practice and share ideas?

It is highly likely that a mailing list of all the locality, cluster or academy schools you belong to is already set up, so all you have to do is to set a time and place, draft an invitation and ask for it to be circulated.

There are a number of networks which support teachers to engage with evidence and research-based practice. The Chartered College of Teaching is a professional organisation that aims to bridge gaps between research and practice through its articles, blogs and journals, which focus on using evidence-based research to inform excellence in the classroom. Contributions are gathered from a wide range of key and current thinkers and writers in education, helping you to keep informed of new developments in learning and teaching. ResearchEd, an organisation established in 2013, has a particular mission to increase the research literacy of educators so they can engage with and challenge relevant research. Articles are published regularly and events held which allow interested parties to meet and discuss ideas more fully.

Other networks may be more closely focused on specific areas of the curriculum. For example, Teachers as Readers networks share research on developing children as passionate readers. These groups operate across England, run by trained group leaders, and meet to discuss newly published literature to excite and enthuse children. Group members are also encouraged to conduct their own case studies and share their findings on the Open University Research Rich Pedagogies website.

CASE STUDY JOINING A RESEARCH-BASED NETWORK

Harbir is passionate about children's literature so searches for local opportunities to develop his interest further. He discovers there is a Teachers as Readers group based in his local university. The group meets once every half term for an hour after school. There are always recently published books to look at and discuss. There are teachers from different schools so Harbir talks to other people who are as passionate about children's literature as he is. Some are teachers from other local schools, some are librarians who specialise in children's literature and some are trainee teachers who have new ideas to share. The members of the group discuss their perceptions and think about how the books might engage different members of their classes or work well with a particular year group which Harbir can then pass on to his colleagues. There is always some input from the group leaders too, the sharing of a case study involving a teacher who has been looking at ways to engage boys further in reading, or a survey about reading that Harbir can carry out in his own classroom

(Continued)

(Continued)

to help him learn more about the children in his class as readers. By attending the group each half term Harbir invests time in building his knowledge of children's books further, increasing his ability to inspire a love of reading in his pupils.

Explore the Teachers as Readers initiative at the following website:

https://ourfp.org/finding/reading-teachers-teachers-who-read-and-readers-who-teach/

Similar to Harbir, consider the benefits that networks such as these can have on your teaching practice in the primary classroom.

Dedicating time to following your real passions in teaching can help to support job satisfaction. In the case study feature box above you can see how Harbir has developed his sense of professional identity as a teacher who enjoys reading and discussing children's books in a way that has a direct impact on his classroom provision and teaching.

HOW ELSE CAN PROFESSIONAL NETWORKS SUPPORT PRIMARY TEACHERS?

Networks have very good potential for teachers to develop increased knowledge and understanding, widening the pool of knowledge by enabling teachers from different schools to come together. However, through such collaboration networks also offer teachers affective benefits. Frost et al. suggest that *it might be assumed that knowledge-building among teachers is all about passing on know-how but there is another dimension which is essentially concerned with the inspirational value of what is shared* (2018: 155).

Firth suggests that engaging in evidence-based exploration *requires teachers to have control over what they do in the classroom, and so the movement towards teacher research engagement has an intrinsic link to teacher agency* (2018: 20). During their training, prospective primary teachers will have engaged with new and seminal research, considering key theories alongside their classroom practice and exploring how viewing such practice through the lens of key theories supports them in uncovering what makes highly effective practice. Through these experiences, they become conversant with reading research studies and may well have carried out their own enquiries to answer questions that interest them. Thus, engaging with research networks allows new teachers to continue to hone these skills as they deepen their knowledge.

A study of the role of research in teacher education conducted by BERA (2014) found that engaging in research gives teachers some autonomy which is a key factor in job satisfaction, empowering them to better understand how they might enhance their practice and increase their impact through the ongoing process of professional reflection and enquiry. It asserts that this is a key aspect of teachers' identity as professionals, and reinforces other important aspects such as subject knowledge and classroom practice.

Stevenson (2018: 89) suggests that *the ability to exercise judgement, make decisions and act in ways that bring about change in other words, to have, and experience, control* is the agency at the heart of a research-engaged approach to professionalism:

it is fruitful to think about questions of agency and control in relation to professional knowledge and professional learning. Being involved in framing the knowledge base that underpins teaching, and having control over one's own professional learning, can be considered core aspects of teacher professionalism.

(2018: 89)

However, it is not just research-based networks which can make a valuable contribution to teachers' sense of well-being. Weston and Clay (2018) identify a connection between professional learning and teachers' morale, sense of efficacy and motivation, and Amabile and Kramer (2011) found that the ability to make meaningful changes is highly motivating and prompts creativity in the workplace. Maslach and Leiter take the view that *when employees have the perceived capacity to influence decisions that affect their work, to exercise professional autonomy, and to gain access to the resources necessary to do an effective job, they are more likely to experience job engagement* (2016: 105).

Maintaining a sense of autonomy at work offers a chance to reconnect to values, highlighting the importance of choosing goals, teaching methods and educational strategies that reflect personal educational philosophies (Skaavlik and Skaavlik, 2014). Maslach and Leiter recognise the importance of these values as *the ideals and motivations that originally attracted people to their job, and thus they are the motivating connection between the worker and the workplace* (2016: 105).

THEORY FOCUS SELF-DETERMINATION THEORY

Self-determination theory considers what underpins a person's self-motivation and which conditions support it to flourish. Ryan and Deci (2000) view people as having a natural desire to grow, to seek novelty and challenge, to explore and to learn. This desire is referred to as intrinsic motivation; all people find particular activities rewarding or satisfying in themselves because they are enjoyable or interesting.

Ryan and Deci propose that intrinsic motivation is underpinned by three basic psychological needs: competence, the ability to perform successfully; relatedness, a feeling of being connected to people or things; and autonomy, the feeling of engaging in activity of your own choice. So, activities which fulfil a person's need for competence, relatedness and autonomy support a person's intrinsic motivation and enhance a sense of well-being.

Ryan and Deci suggest that any basic need is *an energizing state that, if satisfied, conduces toward health and well-being but, if not satisfied, contributes to pathology and ill-being* (2000: 74). In a recent article on teacher well-being, Crome and Cise (2020) propose that paying attention to the three psychological needs that underpin intrinsic motivation has the potential to increase the well-being of teachers.

Autonomy is not only of benefit to teachers. Ryan and Deci cite a number of studies which have shown that teachers who value and support autonomy in their pupils, promote *greater intrinsic motivation, curiosity, and desire for challenge* in their own pupils (2000: 70-1). Interestingly, this would appear to support teachers in working through aspects of the behaviour component of the Early Career Framework: *helping pupils to journey from needing extrinsic motivation to being motivated to work intrinsically* (DfE, 2019c: 23).

In his study of early career teachers, Roness (2011) explored teachers' motivation and found that teachers' reasons for entering the profession were primarily intrinsic, focused on the joy of teaching, or altruistic, focused on social justice with a desire to contribute to the growth and development of pupils. Therefore, participating in networks which enable teachers to pursue passions and interests, and that align with their values, offers benefits to both the development of professional knowledge and to teachers' motivation (Guerriero, 2014).

There are a number of networks which seek to bring together teachers to share their thinking in informal ways, thus contributing to the fulfilment of competence, relatedness and autonomy. One of these is a TeachMeet, an event which encourages teachers to present effective classroom practice with one another. Typically, these events are organised into small time slots of around seven minutes, where any teacher can share what they've been working on. Some TeachMeets have a specific focus: for example, the whole event may be about Special Educational Needs, a particular curriculum subject, or an aspect of one such as vocabulary development, or be phase specific. Some schools or clusters will also offer their own informal networks such as journal clubs where members agree to read and discuss interesting articles.

CLASSROOM LINK BUILDING NETWORKS THAT MATTER TO YOU

Think about the opportunities you know of to get involved with networks. Are there any local ones that you have heard of or could search for? Are there particular areas of the curriculum that interest you which have subject associations you could get involved with? Are there particular values that drew you into teaching and which you are keen to maintain a connection to? Might you find out about the Chartered College for Teaching or ResearchEd and visit their websites to find out more? Perhaps you could join, or even start, a journal club? Revisit the table you drew earlier on and make notes on what you could do to involve yourself in one or more networks

CHAPTER SUMMARY

How might professional networks benefit teachers both personally and professionally?

There are a number of networks that can support the development of professional knowledge, offer opportunities to connect with teachers across the profession and that have the potential to increase some aspects of teachers' sense of well-being in order to ensure that collectively members of the profession provide the very best education for their pupils.

This chapter has considered how involvement in such networks can support teachers in their ongoing development as highly effective professionals.

━ **ASSIGNMENT LINKS** ━━━━━━━━━━━━━━━━━━━━━━━━━━━━

Most assignments require secondary reading to substantiate or evidence the points made within arguments. As you plan your assignments, explore what articles, research evidence and subject principles can be sourced via ResearchEd, Chartered College for Teaching and Council of Subject Associations. Website links are provided in the further reading below. Find out the costs to join these networks (often free or reduced for early career teachers) so that you have access to the widest range of materials that can inform your assignments.

━━━━ **FURTHER READING** ━━━━━━━━━━━━━━━━━━━━━━━

The Chartered College of Teaching: https://chartered.college/ *publish a number of concise, easy-to-read articles on all aspects of learning and teaching written by a wide range of authors. You can search for specific themes, read their most recent publications, or join their journal club.*

ResearchEd: https://researched.org.uk/ *publish a monthly magazine (available in print and online) with focused articles on a wide range of education-related topics.*

The Council for Subject Associations: https://www.subjectassociations.org.uk/ *maintains an up-to-date directory of useful contacts organised by subject. The news section of the website provides useful updates related to learning and teaching.*

7

HOW CAN PRIMARY TEACHERS DEVELOP THEIR PROFESSIONALISM ONLINE?

LINDA COOPER AND DEBRA LAXTON

KEY WORDS: SOCIAL MEDIA; PERSONAL LEARNING NETWORK; DIGITAL FOOTPRINT; SAFETY; PROFESSIONAL DEVELOPMENT; INTERNET

INTRODUCTION

This chapter explores the potential of the virtual landscape for the development of a teacher's professional growth. The internet, particularly social media, offers numerous opportunities for the educator and is an increasingly prevalent activity. The following discussion will explore the benefits of social media and considers how this can be harnessed to help teachers be more effective. Additionally, this chapter explores the notion of a digital footprint. As with most initiatives, new ways of working bring both opportunity and risk. The pitfalls associated with social media will be discussed and we will examine how and why teachers need to keep themselves safe online.

WHAT DO WE MEAN BY THE TERM 'SOCIAL MEDIA'?

The Cambridge English Dictionary (2020) defines social media as: *websites and computer programs that allow people to communicate and share information on the internet using a computer or mobile phone.*

Typical applications that are employed as social media devices include:

- Facebook
- Twitter
- Snapchat
- Instagram
- LinkedIn
- Pinterest
- YouTube.

The above are just a few suggestions of different types of social media. These applications are also augmented by educationalists that produce wikis, blogs and vlogs on hundreds of educational subjects.

CLASSROOM LINK

Consider the presence and influence of social media in your life. Is it a dominant force or more of a background feature that offers the occasional opportunity? Write down all the different types of social media that you use for your professional development. Now move down the page and divide it in half. For each application, on one side of the page try to record the potential advantages of its use for your professional growth. On the other side, consider any disadvantages. After you have read this chapter revisit your original list and add any additional new information you have acquired.

WHAT ARE THE BENEFITS OF USING SOCIAL MEDIA FOR DEVELOPING A PROFESSIONAL PROFILE?

The beginning of a teaching career is an exciting but challenging time. It is exhilarating to have responsibility of your own class of children. It is full of opportunity but at the same time it can be filled with questions for which you might not have the answers and you can feel 'marooned'. You have your colleagues as useful sources of information, but you may feel that they are sometimes too busy to help and the virtual landscape now offers another potential route for inspiration. Social media allows the educator to overcome geographical, temporal and hierarchical boundaries and can reduce the isolation that can be associated with teaching (Carpenter and Harvey, 2020).

Teachers collaborate with a huge number of like-minded individuals. The opportunity to engage in professional dialogue is now no longer limited to your immediate school or 'school-cluster' but can occur virtually at a national and international level. Engaging in online dialogue broadens the perspective and can offer a multiplicity of different views on any given educational discourse. This is important for our professional development as growth depends on this type of engagement as opposed to listening to a small group of similar views that may exist in one school. Glazzard and Mitchell (2018: 78) support this endeavour stating: *Social media spaces provide opportunities for groups with similar interests or challenges from across the country and the world to share their experiences for others to draw on.*

Importantly, they also refer to social media creating 'communities of practice' (Wenger, 1998) where collective knowledge helps to advise on common issues in education.

CRITICAL QUESTION

How can social media be used to fill gaps in teacher subject knowledge?

To be an effective educator we have to continue to be curious, interested and a lifelong learner. Social media can strengthen our professional development in several ways, particularly in relation to understanding and resourcing the curriculum. Secure subject knowledge is important in helping us to become effective practitioners. For the primary teacher this can be a continual endeavour. Most immediately, social media can provide access to a fruitful source of ideas across the curriculum to develop classroom practice. Creating a post on social media asking for ideas in a particular subject area can create quick and numerous responses. The professional has moved from a position where it was often difficult to find resources to one where we have a potential mass of information that needs to be evaluated and deciphered. Cranefield and Yoong (2009) argue that a less recognised benefit of using the diverse range of tools offered by social media such as blogs, wikis and messaging is that they help to deepen understanding of a topic as teachers are required to continually rephrase knowledge on a subject so that it is well adapted to the specifics of each different communication context.

CASE STUDY USING SOCIAL MEDIA TO BRIDGE GAPS IN SUBJECT KNOWLEDGE

Early career teacher Shiv was scheduled to teach the Iron Age to his Key Stage 2 class, but felt he lacked sufficient subject knowledge in this area of the curriculum. To action this knowledge deficit he took responsibility for bridging this gap in his prior learning by using social media. His first steps involved investigating his locality to ascertain potential places of interest that he could take his class to visit to help them build context for the Iron Age. He then sought to improve his subject knowledge using online content. He started to follow relevant museums via their social media accounts and discovered that they offered virtual visits. If the school's budget did not support the funds necessary to visit in person, he could also potentially arrange for an Iron Age experience to come to their classroom. This provided two opportunities. First, the children would gain an exciting experience and the visit would make the learning memorable. Second, he would present them with the opportunity to question potential subject experts in this curriculum area. Through regular tweets from his local museum, Shiv discovered that they were offering free online evening lectures about the Iron Age. By attending these lectures he was able to listen to a researcher in this field discuss their findings, which improved his own subject knowledge significantly. While attending the lecture he was able to pose questions for discussion.

To continue his development Shiv knew that subject associations were a good place to help with both content and pedagogical knowledge-building. As well as browsing the relevant subject association's website Shiv also started to follow their Twitter posts, taking particular note of any that were associated with the Iron Age. From this he observed that certain individuals were key players in contributing to, and reflecting on, discussions and were also acting as experts in their field. On closer inspection he found that these individuals had their own websites through which they provided content that could be shared with the online community – this ranged from exemplar lesson plans to YouTube clips where teachers articulated their views on other potential of resources or explained their own lesson ideas. Shiv made sure he bookmarked all of these useful websites.

In a short space of time Shiv found that by using digital tools he quickly resourced an engaging set of ideas on the Iron Age period.

┏━ CLASSROOM LINK ━━━┓

After reading the above case study, consider a topic that you might need further support with. Can you source online subject associations, local interest groups or primary school professionals who are producing social media/online material?

PERSONAL LEARNING NETWORKS

As well as being a good conduit for information gathering, Thompson (2018) discusses social media in more aspirational terms. She views social media as an educational movement that has changed professional growth. No longer does a practitioner have to wait for professional development opportunities to occur via dedicated centres or conferences, for example, nor do restricted budget implications act as a barrier to opportunity. Instead, teachers can take control of the growth of their own skills and knowledge. Carpenter and Harvey (2020) note that most professional activities using social media are carried out voluntarily but the fact that it is so popular intrinsically shows its value. Thompson (2018: 4) argues that *becoming a teacher who is actively involved in a program of self-directed sustained professional development is one of the wisest decisions you can make as a novice educator.*

Thompson (2018) and Trust (2012) further explore the concepts of professionalism and view social media in terms of professional 'learning' via the creation of a 'personal learning network' (PLN). A PLN is a defined as a series of connections and resources that can be used for informal learning and collaboration to exchange knowledge (Trust, 2012). Gradually, PLNs become embedded in a teacher's daily use to help improve both subject knowledge and understanding of pedagogy (Trust, 2012).

Marcia and Garcia (2016) investigated personal learning networks and found that they could be advantageous in helping to establish interactions between teachers at different stages in their careers, particularly pre-service teachers and in-service practitioners. This form of interaction could encourage virtual 'mentor'-like relationships that emulated practices that occur in physical classroom situations. Marcia and Garcia (2016) note that the reciprocal nature of these relationships was an asset for both the actors in the relationship and for the profession in general. New practitioners could ask for advice from fellow teachers and experts and by doing so gain in confidence while experienced teachers had an opportunity to reflect on their practice. These participants also noted that the potential anonymity of social media platforms helped teachers to share concerns and anxieties or consult on problematic situations to gain support.

The examination of Shiv's quest for subject knowledge development – explained in the previous case study – shows that he was, in actual fact, developing a PLN. Establishing, maintaining and then consulting a PLN helps in the more efficient collection of, and quick access to, professional resources like digital books, articles, blogs, videos and podcasts. Tour (2017) describes these types of activities as one of the key professional practices achieved via a PLN. She also discusses how the collection of professional resources needs to be organised in a meaningful fashion using digital tools like social bookmarking. The classification of these materials encourages teachers to reflect on and evaluate resources and helps them to transform the information from a collection of disparate artefacts into useful knowledge. It also encourages the further sharing of information. For instance, using social bookmarking services facilitates the further sharing of resources via the PLN.

As well as providing a place for collating resources and gaining advice from others, it is suggested that PLNs provide an unexpected opportunity to socialise. Teachers have described how PLNs have provided an outlet to talk about different aspects of their life and work with people who face similar challenges and environments. Some report meeting members of their PLN both virtually and physically in a face-to-face situation, and describe how this has offered a source of new, collegiate relationships and professional friendships (Tour, 2017).

CRITICAL QUESTION

How do you use social media? Do you contribute content or do you like to observe information supplied by others?

Read the Theory focus and consider the different categories of user.

THEORY FOCUS

Prestridge (2019) conducted a small, international research project exploring teacher use of social media for their professional learning. For this investigation, research methods involved interviewing ICT specialist teachers to discuss their professional learning outside school-based opportunities and to analyse online engagements that moved beyond general expressions of using social media to share content. The research sample involved teachers from three different countries across the globe. These included Queensland in Australia, Belgium in Europe and Indiana in the USA. Themes associated with professional learning were categorised into a working typology populated by four distinct strands based on how the participants described and enacted their own use of social media.

Category 1: info-consumer. These users employ social media as a resource bank and as a virtual space that can be utilised to gain ideas. Users 'follow' a large number of content providers in a certain area of the curriculum to stay up to date with ideas. They keep abreast of new ideas as they appear on social media, but do not participate in discussion or add their own content.

Category 2: info-networker. The main difference between this category and the info-consumer is that the info-networker uses social media to gain ideas and then subsequently shares these with colleagues in their own educational establishment. These users actively seek to follow educators they value to discover effective sources of information to share.

Category 3: self-seeking contributor. These participants actively provide content to social media sites. This might be in the form of exchanging ideas, contributing knowledge or even curriculum materials. They do this to receive feedback on the content provided or to validate their ideas. These users might participate in social media when they have a problem or question or to confirm that a certain course of action will be effective. By doing this they effectively use a PLN to develop understanding of their own capabilities.

Category 4: vocationalist. These participants are motivated to engage with social media to build a learning community. They might start a conversation and take the lead in proposing new ideas for comment. They might use this network to gather other resources and regularly share them. They will be active in how they contribute to a variety of platforms and wish to engage regularly with their knowledge-building community. People might follow them and they would be considered leaders in a certain field.

CRITICAL QUESTION

Does social media play a role in accessing the most recent educational developments?

ACCESS TO RESEARCH

Use of social media and a PLN helps a teacher keep abreast of important developments in education. Good professional growth requires a teacher to stay research informed. For many teachers this intention is usually a sound aspiration, but achieving this aim can be problematic when dealing with the complexities and pressures of classroom life. Moreover, attendance at research-informed educational conferences can be hindered by geographical and economic barriers. The use of social media provides access to conference content as speakers and participants tend to use platforms like Twitter or micro-blogging facilities to share information. This trend was particularly important during the global COVID-19 pandemic.

Social media also plays an increasingly important role in helping research reach a wider audience. Traditionally, the timeline for the publication of high-quality, peer-reviewed research is lengthy and access to journal information has relied on a teacher being able to access a university library. This is changing. Journals are now available via community-curated, online directories developed to increase the visibility, accessibility and impact of high-quality research. Moreover, researchers now use social media as a conduit to access potential groups of educators who might participate in, or evaluate, ongoing research. They might also use social media to urgently disseminate their work. The following theory focus describes this phenomenon in more detail.

THEORY FOCUS USING SOCIAL MEDIA TO REACH A WIDE AUDIENCE DURING THE COVID-19 PANDEMIC

The University of Chichester led the creation of a free and easily accessible electronic 'Parent's guide to promoting early learning and development at home' (Laxton, 2020). The guide was specifically designed to support families with young children isolated at home due to the coronavirus pandemic during the spring 2020 national lockdown in England. The document follows the principles and content of England's Early Years Foundation Stage framework (DfE, 2017b). It initially outlines the value and significance of play-based learning and then offers tips and advice related to each of the seven areas of learning.

A digital technology-driven dissemination strategy was essential to ensure scale and speed of access to the guide. A key element of the strategy was to target a wide variety of relevant digital platforms simultaneously by providing a guide rationale together with a one-click weblink to the resource. Known contacts and networks within the Early Years education sector, working directly with settings and parents, were targeted. Due to the pandemic, digital technologies were being used to enable communication with parents to continue and it was assumed that educators would want to share

(Continued)

(Continued)

reliable, helpful information for parents to promote home learning and this would enable traction by raising awareness of the guide.

1. A website was created to provide a platform for the digital guide https://www.skipforeyeducators. co.uk/. A single click on a link directed individuals straight to the downloadable guide.

2. The University of Chichester website and local press covered the launch of the guide.

3. The following networks/media channels were used to communicate simultaneously.

   - The internet was used to source local authority contacts and emails were subsequently sent to 49 local authority Children's Services across England. Local authorities then shared the link with schools and Early Years settings in their specific areas via email, Facebook and Twitter.

   - Personal learning networks were used, e.g. posts by the author on personal and professional Facebook accounts, tweets on Twitter, university Early Years network members each received emails. Posts were re-shared and educators shared the weblink directly with parents.

   - Posts were made to popular Early Years education and parenting Facebook pages, e.g. Keeping Early Years Unique (KEYU), Early Education, Education Endowment Foundation. The KEYU post alone received 267 comments and 348 likes demonstrating the positive response.

Speed and response rates show that dissemination was effective. The guide was accessed 40,000 times in the three weeks that followed its launch and it continues to be accessed regularly. Although the rate has slowed, an average rate of 2,000 downloads per month persists. As of February 2021, there had been over 74,000 downloads. The case study shows how effectively digital technologies and social media in particular, but also more traditional technologies such as emails, can be used to share work quickly, easily and widely with interested parties using personal learning networks and the internet to source and target a specific audience. The timely publication of the resource, shortly after 'lockdown', alongside a motivation of the guide authors and Early Years educators to support families in a unique 'stay at home' situation were certainly significant contributory factors in explaining the popularity of the resource. However, it is national technology readiness levels and the technology knowledge and skills of educators and parents that enabled the access.

WHY IS IT IMPORTANT TO OBSERVE APPROPRIATE BOUNDARIES WITH SCHOOL COMMUNITIES?

CRITICAL QUESTION

What is a digital footprint? Can you have a positive or negative digital foot print?

Teachers are role models for their communities and therefore need to adhere to professional standards of conduct; this applies to both their physical role in a school and their online presence. It is easy for boundaries to be blurred in the online world and this can have unfortunate consequences. Thompson

(2018: 70) considers this strand of professionalism to be of high importance, noting that *Few things can ruin a teacher's professional reputation and affect the way your colleagues regard you more quickly than indiscrete content on a social media site.*

It is useful to remember that our discourses and presence online need to meet the same standards that would apply to professional dialogue within the physical environment of a school. We need to be aware of our digital footprint and consider what our internet usage says about us as professionals.

Each time we use the internet we leave a mark that indicates a visit to that page – all of this can be collected together to create our 'digital footprint'. It is difficult to track our complete browsing history, but our social media footprint can, and should be, managed. Teachers need to consider what their internet usage says about their character. Posting poorly chosen pictures and comments on social media can lead to the creation of a negative digital footprint that will cause others to form an undesirable impression of that individual and impact on employment potential. Poor choices for online behaviour can also expose the school that currently employs that person to negative reputational impacts and a decrease in trust with the community.

The way we respond to discussion threads on social media is also key. Posting critical comments using aggressive language in a professional online discussion can be detrimental. It is worth acknowledging that posting in anger is not a good decision; we need to manage our online emotional dispositions just as we would expect to do in the physical world. Attention needs to be focused on the creation of a positive professional footprint that shows a good digital character and positive role modelling. Glazzard and Mitchell (2018) note that schools should help staff in this endeavour by agreeing a code of conduct that is informed by a simple set of guidelines to be agreed and followed by all pupils and staff. These guidelines should avoid the use of overly complicated language, but should introduce terms like 'digital footprint' to create a shared vocabulary of safe online practice. The code of conduct should encourage students and staff to consider the consequences of actions and encourage a positive online presence.

HOW CAN STUDENT TEACHERS PROTECT THEIR ONLINE IDENTITIES AS THEY BEGIN AND MOVE THROUGH THEIR INITIAL TEACHER EDUCATION?

Teachers need to teach children digital citizenship skills and also attend to the management of their own digital life. The following points could be useful to adhere to.

- Educators need to protect their identity by carefully managing the privacy settings of their social media accounts. Many social media platforms will set an account to public by default. By managing privacy settings on social media you can control who will see posts.

- Do not give out personal information about yourself or others online.

- When installing apps, notice that they may request permission to use your data. Consider what personal information it is accessing and check the privacy policy to establish what it uses the data for.

- Check the settings to verify what access other users of that app may have to your personal information and other data.

- Consider all your posts as public information even if you have attended to the privacy settings on your social media account and have controlled who can see posts. All pictures and information posted can be easily copied or screenshot and passed on without your permission or knowledge.

- Use the school's social media accounts to communicate information to parents and children rather than personal accounts.

- Be aware of school policies and any codes of conduct related to your online presence and adhere to these.

- Look at your 'friends' list on your social media accounts and ensure that you 'know' all of your contacts. Consider carefully who you ask to be a friend or from whom you accept friendship requests.

CASE STUDY SOCIAL MEDIA DILEMMAS

Year 6 teacher Susan was a keen social media user. She was aware of the need to act responsibly and maintain her privacy by keeping personal and professional social media accounts separate. Despite managing her platforms some ex-pupils had tried to contact her via a personal account, asking to be accepted as a 'friend'. Susan declined these requests. Last week she had received a request from a teaching assistant colleague. The teaching assistant was not part of the team who worked in Susan's class and she had never taught any of her three children; she liked and respected this person. Susan did not know whether to accept her request but did not want to upset her by declining.

- How should Susan deal with this situation?

- Are some social media platforms more suited to professional networking than others?

THEORY FOCUS HIDDEN IMPLICATIONS OF SOCIAL MEDIA PLATFORM USE

Bergviken Rensfeldt et al. (2018) argue that empirical literature to date has tended to frame educators' use of social media for professional growth as relatively unproblematic. These researchers examined the phenomenon of large-scale communities of educators formed using a social media platform (in this instance Facebook). A case study investigation was undertaken of a large Facebook community developed by Swedish teachers who were all interested in the use of technology to appropriate 'flipped learning' strategies. Flipped learning requires a student to engage with content before they experience the associated 'lesson' in a face-to-face classroom-based situation. Researchers studied the activity of the group, which consisted of over 13,000 members, over a period of three years. They distributed a survey to members collecting data about their use of the group. Data was also collected through a focus group and via a set of longer interviews carried out with the moderator of the virtual community.

Findings highlighted the many positives for professionals using the group through which they gained useful information and advice to develop their professional knowledge; many of these were examined earlier in the chapter. However, Bergviken Rensfeldt et al. (2018) also considered aspects of use which they described as devaluing and disempowering for the users. These authors draw attention to the fact that Facebook operates by mining and selling data to third parties. The creation of content generated by this group was marketable to advertisers through which they could promote technology products. The research determined that this could be considered exploitative and that users of this type of platform should be aware that when they contributed they were not only working for themselves but unconsciously working for the social media site and advertising companies too. Moreover, the paper finds that in this instance Facebook used a prescriptive technology designed for compliance that reduced decision-making. The interface presented a narrow selection of content to users despite some members' attempts to disrupt the flow of information. The group was therefore characterised by passive interaction and content was determined by the platform's algorithms rather than teacher expertise. The type of interaction on the site was further analysed for its diversity of discussion. It was found that posts were largely devoid of reciprocal discussion and differential in their nature. Posts were noted for their 'sameness', meaning that opportunity for alternative viewpoints were lost.

Finally, Bergviken Rensfeldt et al. (2018) note how professional development of this type was carried out using a substantial amount of personal time instead of using the site during work hours. Using social media sites like this could therefore simply be adding to the notion of over-work and just exacerbate the high demands and stress.

CHAPTER SUMMARY

Why is it important for teachers to consider the online dimension of professionalism? With the growth of both research and social networking opportunities for teachers, it is no longer relevant to think of primary school teachers as individuals in classrooms. There is a vast network of online opportunities to support the professional work of primary teachers. As such, this chapter has considered:

- the theme of professional identity and growth in relation to social media;
- how social media can be harnessed to help you with your professional development;
- personal learning networks that can be formulated to help deepen an understanding of pedagogy, give access to up-to-date information on initiatives in the educational world and enable direct communication with other professionals including experts in any specific field;
- the responsible use of social media, the understanding of digital citizenship and the creation of positive digital footprints; fostering a good digital character is the professional responsibility of all teachers.

ASSIGNMENT LINKS

Assignments that require you to consider your professional values and identity should also link to how this is realised through your online activity. Tasks that ask you to think about online safety should incorporate discussion of both pupils and staff - good digital citizenship should apply to all of the school community.

━━━━━━━━ **FURTHER READING** ━━━━━━━━

Poore, M. (2015) *Using Social Media in the Classroom: A Best Practice Guide.* London: SAGE

This book gives a very good overview of different ways social media can be used.

Thompson, Julia G. (2018) *The First-Year Teacher's Survival Guide: Ready-To-Use Strategies, Tools and Activities for Meeting the Challenges of Each School Day.* Hoboken, NJ: John Wiley & Sons

This book gives simple and realistic advice about all areas of teaching but includes good sections on using the internet for professional development.

8

HOW DO PROFESSIONAL FRAMEWORKS SUPPORT PROFESSIONALISM IN PRIMARY TEACHING?

GLENN STONE

KEYWORDS: EXTENDED PROFESSIONALISM; EQUALITIES ACT; HEALTH AND SAFETY; NATIONAL CURRICULUM; PROFESSIONAL FRAMEWORKS; SAFEGUARDING; WORKLOAD

INTRODUCTION

Throughout this book, references are made to professional frameworks, particularly the Teachers' Standards, Core Content Framework and Early Career Framework. However, a primary teacher has responsibilities related to a whole range of legal and professional frameworks. Some frameworks are local to the school, such as a school's code of conduct; others will be national frameworks, such as the National Curriculum. This chapter looks at some of the frameworks and responsibilities that primary teachers should be aware of. It is divided into three sections that cover: who can work as a primary teacher; how primary teachers look after the interests of children; and the frameworks required for teaching.

WHO CAN WORK AS A PRIMARY SCHOOL TEACHER?

The licence to teach in England is gained through the award of Qualified Teacher Status (QTS). QTS is not a prerequisite for teaching in the independent sector and while academies and free schools are also free to employ unqualified teachers most seek QTS holders when recruiting. While there are alternative ways to certify the work of teachers, England adopts a free market model. The perceived benefits of this model include what Voisin and Dumay (2020: 7) summarise as maximising *the 'fit' between teachers and schools ... Professional and performance standards serve as benchmarks, stressing the importance of monitoring the quality of the teaching workforce along the way.* This means that an employing head teacher can be fairly confident that any teacher who applies for a position will be able to demonstrate a standardised set of knowledge, skills and understanding regardless of their training route or background. To hold QTS, teachers must be able to meet and uphold the Teachers' Standards (DfE, 2011). Within the market model, the role of universities in shaping the profession is not as important as it has been in historical definitions: *The association of universities with professions seems to follow ineluctably, because professions rest on knowledge and universities are the seat of knowledge in modern societies* (Abbott, 1988: 195).

However, with professional training routes no longer requiring substantial university input, the starting point for a newly qualified teacher (NQT) may be seen as moving away from framing teaching as a knowledge-based profession (as in Finland where there is a longer period of initial teacher education). Yet, teachers' subject knowledge has become increasingly dominant in debates surrounding the teaching profession; initial teacher education should not be seen as the end of teachers' professional development, but the start. Recent developments in the Core Content and Early Career frameworks help provide a transition between initial teacher education and the first two years of qualified teaching.

CRITICAL QUESTION

Why is it important that teachers are fit to teach?

Schools must ensure that the children in school are safe. If a teacher is unwell or unable to carry out the duties of a teacher with reasonable adjustments, then they may not be deemed fit to teach. Institutions offering initial teacher education and employing schools may ask an early career teacher or qualified teacher to produce medical evidence that declares them fit to teach. This can involve occupational health and as part of recruitment will usually involve a medical declaration. For example, the Education (Health Standards) Regulations 2003 state that a teacher must be able to plan, prepare and deliver lessons to children. If a teacher has a mental or physical illness that prevents them from being able to carry out those duties, even with reasonable adjustments, then they may not be deemed fit to be in the classroom.

HOW SHOULD PRIMARY TEACHERS SPEND THEIR TIME?

DfE (2020a) signposts the contractual responsibilities of teachers, and many of these responsibilities are closely aligned to the Teachers' Standards. Some of the most relevant responsibilities for early career teachers is set out below:

- plan and teach lessons to their class within the context of the school curriculum;

- assess, monitor, record and report on the learning needs, progress and achievements of assigned pupils;

- contribute to the development, implementation and evaluation of the school's policies, practices and procedures in such a way as to support the school's values and vision;

- work with others on curriculum and/or pupil development to secure coordinated outcomes;

- promote the safety and well-being of pupils;

- maintain good order and discipline among pupils;

- direct and supervise support staff assigned to them;

- deploy resources delegated to them;

- participate and engage with performance appraisal arrangements and professional development;

- communicate with pupils, parents and carers;

- collaborate and work with colleagues and other relevant professionals within and beyond the school.

Unsurprisingly, some of the points above are integral to teaching and learning. Planning, teaching, assessment and behaviour management are all necessary to support individual pupil learning. Other points are aligned to supporting the progress of the school as a whole, such as working with others to secure coordinated outcomes and contributing to school policies. There are also points that can be interpreted as supporting broader aims in society. For example, promoting the safety and well-being of pupils is not just about learner engagement, but can be seen as contributing to the moral health of the nation. Children that are in good physical and mental health are going to put less strain on the National Health Service as they grow older. Teachers that identify safeguarding concerns are supporting the work of social services and the police to maintain order in a society. It is worth considering this point when reading through the following theory focus.

THEORY FOCUS EXTENDED PROFESSIONALISM

Hoyle (1974) argued in favour of an extended form of professionalism. At this time, teachers were perceived to have greater autonomy, free of prescribed curricula, for example. Hoyle argued that this generated a restricted professionalism where teachers concentrated on the teaching and learning of their pupils but did not necessarily need to consider engagement outside their classrooms. Hoyle proposed that teachers should move towards an extended professionalism where they worked collegiately and situated their work within broader social frameworks. Reflecting on this much cited theory, Hoyle (2008: 292) now argues that reforms to education *not only encouraged extended professionalism, but required it*. When examining the current responsibilities of primary school teachers the wider societal expectations are very much embedded in the work that is carried out. Safeguarding, for example, is of utmost importance and relates the work of teachers to other parallel professions.

CRITICAL QUESTION

Why is it important for teachers to manage their workload?

The 'School teachers' pay and conditions' (DfE, 2020a) states that full-time teachers should be directed to work 1,265 hours per year. For part-time teachers, this will be proportionate to their contract. In addition to the directed hours:

> a teacher must work such reasonable additional hours as may be necessary to enable the effective discharge of the teacher's professional duties, including in particular planning and preparing courses and lessons; and assessing, monitoring, recording and reporting on the learning needs, progress and achievements of assigned pupils.

(DfE, 2020a: 49)

It is important for teachers to consider the implications of these guidelines carefully. A teacher workload survey (DfE, 2019b) shows that primary teachers work, on average, 50 hours per week. Furthermore, Education Support (2020) finds that excessive workload was reported by 62 per cent of teachers who cited work-related reasons for a decline in their mental health.

Table 8.1 shows how the NEU (2020) summarises the way the 1,265 hours per year could be broken down.

Table 8.1   Breakdown of workload (NEU, 2020)

Use of hours	Number of hours	Number of hours per year
Registration	0.25 hours × 190 days	47.5
Mid-session break	0.25 hours × 190 days	47.5
Teaching and PPA time	25 hours per week	950
INSET days	5 hours × 5 days	25
Supervisory duties	0.5 hours × 190 days	95
Parents' meetings/open evenings	3 hours × 3 days	9
Staff meetings	1 hour × 38 days	38
Other duties (e.g. emails)	0.25 hours × 190 days	47.5
Contingency (unforeseen circumstances)	5.5 hours per year (if needed)	5.5
TOTAL		1,265 hours

Keeping to the directed hours is far from straightforward. While there have been suggestions by teaching unions to keep a diary of workload, it is also important to recognise that some teachers choose to work additional hours willingly. For example, an artistic and creative teacher who takes pride in producing displays may choose to spend additional hours setting up the learning environment at the start of term. This may not be directed by the head teacher, but could be something that a teacher does because they get enjoyment out of producing an engaging learning environment. Similarly, a teacher may feel that they want to spend longer on planning lessons or preparing resources, not because they have been told to do so, but because they are worried about not being ready to teach when faced with children in front of them. Evetts (2009) notes how professionalism is sometimes equated to the amount of time that is dedicated. She invites us to think about the professional musician, who would not feel it was out of the ordinary to practise their instrument in order to demonstrate competence and perform at a professional standard. That is not to say that the professional teacher is one who works around the clock. Rather, it is imperative to consider why the hours are being given to the role. If a teacher is being directed by a head teacher to write copious comments on children's written work, then this may not be seen as being important. However, if a primary teacher enjoys spending their free time reading up on a topic that is to be taught because they have an intrinsic love of learning, then this is clearly very different.

HOW DO PRIMARY TEACHERS PROTECT THE INTERESTS OF THE CHILDREN IN THEIR CLASSROOMS?

SAFEGUARDING

Safeguarding children has become a key responsibility of professionals working in primary schools. While it is recognised that everyone has a responsibility to safeguard children (DfE, 2021a), the primary school teacher is a significant person in a child's life. For a child who may be abused or neglected, school should be seen as a safe environment. Teachers must be trained to identify children who will benefit from early help; to do this teachers must know the procedures of their school for reporting concerns. It is the responsibility of employers to ensure their staff are trained in safeguarding. In a primary school safeguarding will be an agenda item for governors' meetings, staff will receive regular updates on changes to government guidance, visitors to a school will be told what to do if they have any concerns while on the premises. All early career teachers should familiarise themselves with the latest version of 'Keeping children safe in education' (DfE, 2021a) and ensure they are familiar with the safeguarding practices in school.

As a primary school teacher, it is important to know how to identify the signs of children who may be at risk of harm. These children will need early help. Primary teachers need to remember that harms can come online as well, whether that is through smartphones, other digital devices or online video gaming communities. Head teachers have a duty to follow safer recruitment guidelines. Classroom teachers need to also be mindful about who may be coming into school as volunteers. That does not mean that teachers need to be suspicious of every volunteer, but it is important that every adult in school is aware of expectations around safeguarding. It is possible that a child could disclose something to a volunteer helper with reading, for example. Procedures for safeguarding should be shared with these volunteers. The key principle is that primary teachers need to get early help to a child who is being harmed or at risk of harm.

As explored in Chapter 1 of this volume, professional occupations are often considered to make a valuable contribution to wider society. When it comes to safeguarding pupils, this is both a short- and long-term aim. For children that are at risk, their immediate lives could be positively impacted by a teacher who notices something and passes on information in the appropriate way. In the longer term, the way that teachers provide a safe environment and act as an appropriate role model can help shape the way that children see themselves and the adults they will become. Primary school teachers are particularly important in this regard as they have more continuous contact with children than any other adult outside a child's family. Knowing how to spot the signs of a child in need and supporting all children to become healthy, active citizens is a moral imperative.

PREVENT DUTY

The Prevent strategy is a UK initiative to *reduce the threat to the UK from terrorism by stopping people becoming terrorists or supporting terrorism* (Home Office, 2019). The strategy has some variation for the devolved nations, but the overarching aims remain the same. The Prevent strategy is part of a wider counter-terrorism (CONTEST) strategy and is also included in schools' broader safeguarding duties.

Any child could become radicalised; radicalisation is not specific to a particular religion, faith or group. However, for some children the risks are greater. Primary school-aged children are not immune from the risks. Some children may be targeted from an early age and older children may be targeted by gangs or others. However, as most primary school children are taught predominantly by a single teacher there is a chance that signs of radicalisation can be identified more easily, particularly if there is a change in behaviour. The NSPCC (2021) argues that radicalisation is difficult to spot, but some signs include:

- a child isolating themselves from family and friends;

- a child talking as if from a scripted speech;

- a child showing unwillingness or inability to discuss their views;

- a sudden disrespectful attitude towards others;

- increased levels of anger in a child;

- a child demonstrating increased secretiveness, especially around internet use.

Many aspects of the typical primary school ethos already support the aims of Prevent. For example, schools have a long-established duty to promote community cohesion. This is also an important facet of professionalism. Professionals in the public sector provide a service that works to the benefit of broader society. If a school sees itself as being integral to the local community, then effective teachers working under effective leaders will already promote community cohesion.

The Prevent strategy also reminds us that *publicly-funded schools in England are required by law to teach a broad and balanced curriculum which promotes the spiritual, moral, cultural, mental and physical development of pupils and prepares them for the opportunities, responsibilities and experiences of life* (Home Office, 2019). In this way, the curriculum, without needing to explicitly address 'radicalisation', is playing a part in helping a young person to contribute positively to society. Whatever the curriculum design, primary teachers should aim to boost children's self-esteem and confidence.

CLASSROOM LINK

You notice that a child has become withdrawn in class. The standard of their work has declined and contributions to class are not as frequent or coherent as they once were. How would you respond? Think about: who you could speak to about this; how to approach the child about your concern; and also, any classroom activities that may support the child.

EQUALITIES ACT

The Equalities Act 2010 lists nine protected characteristics: sex, race, religion or belief, sexual orientation, gender reassignment, pregnancy and maternity, age, disability, marriage and civil partnership. Primary teachers should be aware of their duty not to discriminate. While pregnancy and maternity, and marriage and civil partnership are not typical considerations with working with primary-aged children, it is important not to discriminate against the families and broader community around the school. It is also possible to discriminate by association. NHS England (2020) suggests that the average age for referrals for gender dysphoria is in mid-adolescence. Therefore, although issues surrounding gender reassignment are going to be more prevalent for secondary schools, it is important to recognise that there are primary children who may be questioning their gender identity and this requires sensitivity on the part of a teacher. The Equalities Act 2010 also makes clear that the protected characteristic of age only applies to employment in schools. Therefore, primary teachers need to be particularly aware of their duties not to discriminate against the other characteristics.

Discrimination can occur directly or indirectly. Direct discrimination occurs when an individual sets out to treat someone less favourably than others. Indirect discrimination occurs when the policies and practice are applied to everyone equally, but end up having a disproportionate effect on a group with a shared protected characteristic.

CASE STUDY

A Year 4 teacher wants to take their class on a science field trip to the local woods. In the class, there is a child who uses a wheelchair. The teacher conducts a risk assessment and, after looking at the school's health and safety policy, decides that the terrain is too dangerous for the wheelchair user to access. Therefore, the Year 4 teacher asks the child to remain at school with a teaching assistant to complete science worksheets instead. The remainder of the class attends the field trip.

- Could the Year 4 teacher be accused of direct or indirect discrimination?
- What would you hope the Year 4 teacher has done before making the decisions?
- Could there be a different decision or outcome?

Cases of discrimination are complex and it is unrealistic for a primary school teacher to possess the legal case law that will help inform all the decisions that are taken on a day-to-day basis. In the example above, it would be useful for the teacher to talk to senior leaders in the school about the practicalities of the proposed trip. Through risk assessments, teachers should seek out ways to make reasonable adjustments to the trip and support mechanisms to ensure that every child can take part. The school's outdoor visit policy should also be reviewed to make sure that it is not indirectly discriminating against any groups. The teacher could explore whether there is another part of the woods that is more accessible or whether an alternative experience could be provided to the class in a different way.

WHAT FRAMEWORKS DO PRIMARY TEACHERS NEED TO CONSIDER FOR TEACHING?

LOCAL FRAMEWORKS

Every school will have its own set of policies and procedures. Policies are typically accessible on the school website; further guidance documents may also be available within the school. The local frameworks that a primary teacher needs to be aware of include, but are not limited to:

- the content of the school curriculum, including religious education and the phonics or reading schemes used;

- the behaviour policy;

- policies that outline how additional funding should be used, including the pupil premium and the PE and sport premium;

- the complaints procedure and the school's code of conduct for staff;

- assessment frameworks;

- planning expectations;

- workload and staff well-being policies.

NATIONAL CURRICULUM

In local authority-maintained schools the National Curriculum is a statutory framework that contains the programmes of study for primary teaching. Schools outside local authority control are free to opt out of the National Curriculum, but it remains an ambitious curriculum that is recommended by government. Furthermore, all state schools including academies and free schools must deliver the National Curriculum tests (colloquially referred to as SATs), regardless of the curriculum that they deliver.

One of the aims of the National Curriculum is to provide pupils with *an introduction to the essential knowledge they need to be educated citizens. It introduces pupils to the best that has been thought and said, and helps engender an appreciation of human creativity and achievement* (DfE, 2013). In primary schooling, it is not clear how the content of the National Curriculum achieves this aim. For example, while the English National Curriculum refers to 'classic poetry', there are no prescribed poets, nor is any canon of literature specified. While it can be inferred that this should be the case based on the aim to pass on what its architects have deemed to be *the best that has been thought and said*, professional teachers still have autonomy in making decisions over the texts that they share with their individual classes.

Carr and Skinner (2009) argue that teachers need to move beyond a competency model of their profession and towards a position where teachers are better connected to their social, historical and cultural roots. This is a particular concern for primary school teachers who they believe *lack the wider cultural literacy required for effective promotion of the deeper normative dimensions of human growth and development* (2009: 152). Their argument considers how aspects of the professional teachers' role, such as maintaining discipline, does not necessarily rely upon an engagement with pedagogical theories, but instead can be achieved through a better understanding of human beings. They argue that this understanding can come from reading a wide range of literature and having an appreciation for history and culture. It is a compelling argument that concludes *the most effective teachers are not those who simply regard the acquisition of knowledge and understanding as worthwhile for others, but those who have first and foremost grasped its value for their own personal, moral and spiritual development* (2009: 153). When considering the professionalism of primary teachers, it is worth asking whether curriculum frameworks are followed out of necessity (i.e others expect the National Curriculum to be followed), or whether the curriculum acts a springboard for the professional primary teacher to engage with their own personal cultural education. Therefore, the primary teacher who is able to identify *the best that has been thought and said* is likely to be the teacher who has strong subject knowledge and a cultural wisdom that is able to make connections to the lives of the children that they teach.

INCLUSION AND SPECIAL EDUCATIONAL NEEDS AND DISABILITIES

The National Curriculum states:

Teachers should set high expectations for every pupil. They should plan stretching work for pupils whose attainment is significantly above the expected standard. They have an even greater obligation to plan lessons for pupils who have low levels of prior attainment or come from disadvantaged backgrounds.

(DfE, 2013: 8)

This inclusion statement is a useful starting point for separating the ideas of inclusion and Special Educational Needs and Disability (SEND). As is made clear, all teachers are responsible for the outcomes of their pupils. While it is effective professional practice to work with others where support is required, there cannot be an assumption that it is someone else's role to progress any individual pupil. Inclusion encompasses Special Educational Needs and Disability, but is also an umbrella term for considering all pupils, their backgrounds, their strengths and any barriers that may inhibit them from reaching higher outcomes.

The inclusion statement makes specific reference to children from disadvantaged backgrounds. This group of learners has been the subject of much educational debate, government policy and public spending. For example, the Education Endowment Foundation has received government support to produce research into the link between family income and educational attainment. Schools receive pupil premium funding for disadvantaged pupils, a group predominately comprising children who are or have been eligible for free school meals.

With Special Educational Needs and Disabilities, it is similarly important to ascertain strategies that will support children that need further provision. Primary teachers should know the legislation that is applicable to their role. This is set out in the Code of Practice (DfE/DoHSC, 2015) and includes: the Special Educational Needs and Disability Regulations 2014; the Equality Act 2010; and the Children and Families Act 2014. The Code of Practice shows how each piece of legislation is relevant to the work of teachers.

Often, we hear about 'quality first' teaching, and this is an important starting point. Quality first teaching expects the learning environment, expectations and teaching methods to be inclusive and inspirational for all learners. However, for inexperienced teachers, this can be misinterpreted as an approach that does not need any adaptations for learners. Effective teaching will make adaptations where required. Pupils with Special Educational Needs and Disability will need different adaptations depending on their starting points and barriers. This does not mean that they need to be segregated from the rest of the class and it is important not to set low expectations or make generalisations. As with any other child in the class, it is important to know the child, what they are capable of and the reasons why they may find learning difficult in some areas.

CLASSROOM LINK SPECIAL EDUCATIONAL NEEDS AND THE ROLE OF TEACHING ASSISTANTS

Ms Star is a newly qualified teacher. In her class there are 30 children; five have some form of Special Educational Need at the same time as being lower attaining. The head teacher recommends to Ms Star that she puts those children together on a table with a teaching assistant.

Reflect on the scenario above. Is this arrangement typical in primary schools, or are there alternative ways of directing the teaching assistant? What are the benefits of asking the teaching assistant to support lower-attaining pupils? What are the disadvantages?

The use of teaching assistants to support lower-attaining pupils is often found in primary schools. However, giving over the responsibility for learning to teaching assistants is worth exploring through the lens of professionalism. We can think about the relationship between the role of the teaching assistant and the teacher in a similar way to that of the dental nurse and the dentist. The person with the most training, expertise and professional status should be considered the person best equipped to carry out their role with the specificity required for the task. Within the primary classroom, the 'teacher' is someone who should be responsible for the teaching of all pupils and able to teach those with complex needs. However, as a newly qualified teacher, it is possible that a better job could be carried out by an experienced teaching assistant who has developed a range of skilful strategies to support children over time. Therefore, the qualification of the professional teacher may not compensate for the expertise of the teaching assistant. That being said, the primary teacher needs to be held accountable overall for the children in their class, so it is imperative that they take responsibility for all learning in the classroom. Teachers and teaching assistants need to know how to work together effectively to maximise those learning opportunities, and the teacher needs to ensure that they do not reduce their own input for the pupils who are supported by the teaching assistant.

HEALTH AND SAFETY

The law makes clear what any employee working in a school needs to do with regard health and safety:

- *take reasonable care of their own health and safety and that of others who may be affected by what they do at work;*

- *co-operate with their employers on health and safety matters;*

- *do their work in accordance with training and instructions;*

- *inform the employer of any work situation representing a serious and immediate danger, so that remedial action can be taken.*

(DfE, 2018)

The role of the teacher includes the necessity to keep children safe. Therefore, as part of their professional duties teachers need to become familiar with procedures and regulations that sit outside the principal task of teaching. For example, most primary teachers will be asked to undertake fire safety training on a regular basis. Some teachers may enrol in additional first aid training. Any teacher who is responsible for an off-site visit will need to be familiar with the process of carrying out risk assessments.

As primary teachers tend to teach across the full range of National Curriculum subjects they also need to be familiar with the health and safety considerations linked to subjects, and keep up to date with the latest guidance in this regard. For example, when teaching physical education it is important to know safe techniques for warm-ups and stretches, check that equipment is in a good state of repair and that children know how to carry out physical activities safely.

CHAPTER SUMMARY

Why is it important to adhere to professional frameworks?

This chapter has not provided an exhaustive summary of frameworks that are applicable to primary teachers, but it has provided an entry point for thinking about the connection between the framework and the professional. As professionals, it is important to be competent within these frameworks as primary teachers have professional expectations placed on them through legislation that reflects broader societal expectations of the role.

ASSIGNMENT LINKS

When planning an assignment, spend some time investigating any legislation or professional frameworks that connect to the subject content. For example, an essay on the effective teaching of primary science may consider health and safety legislation and principles of supporting pupils with Special Educational Needs, as well as the National Curriculum expectations.

FURTHER READING

The Bristol Guide: http://www.bristol.ac.uk/education/expertiseandresources/bristolguide/

This provides a comprehensive overview of the statutory frameworks and education legislation. It is produced by, and available from, the University of Bristol.

9

WHAT DOES IT MEAN TO BE ACCOUNTABLE AS A PRIMARY SCHOOL PROFESSIONAL?

GLENN STONE

KEY WORDS: ACCOUNTABILITY; ASSESSMENT; INSPECTION; OFSTED; PERFORMATIVITY; NEOLIBERALISM

INTRODUCTION

Accountability involves holding people responsible for their actions. Someone who can account for their actions is someone who is able to justify why they have acted in a particular way. Accountability can be defined as:

> *The principle of holding people responsible for having participated in, contributed to, or effected an occurrence. To be accountable is to be liable for what has taken place. Accountability often implies obligation and a subsequent expectation to act to counter or explain the behavior for which one is accountable.*

> (Sullivan, 2009)

For schools, this accountability relies on data:

> *[Accountability in education is t]he principle that schools should provide data to show that students are learning the required material and take responsibility for improving student achievement, if necessary. Often, accountability is demonstrated through scores on standardized tests. Schools are then assigned grades or rankings based on results.*

> (Sullivan, 2009)

The two definitions above highlight that there is both internal and external accountability in schools. Internally, individually teachers work within accountability frameworks as part of their contractual duties. They are obligated to carry out the duties expected of a teacher and act accordingly. Externally, the whole school is held to account through a number of measures, including Ofsted reports and comparable performance tables. This chapter will explore both internal and external forms of accountability and what this means for professionals working in primary education.

WHY AND HOW ARE SCHOOLS HELD TO ACCOUNT?

Primary schools working within local authorities are held to account by their local governing bodies and the local authority. Primary schools working as part of a multi-academy trust may also be held to account through localised structures but will, in addition, be accountable directly to the Secretary of State for Education. Regional school commissioners are in place to assist with holding academy schools accountable. For all state-funded schools Ofsted is the school regulator and has an accountability role.

Accountability is accepted to be part of the teaching profession. Research into early career teachers shows an acceptance of accountability as being part of the job (Stone, 2020; Stone-Johnson, 2014). Younger generations of teachers are likely to have spent *their entire educational career in an increasingly performatised school (and higher education) system* (Wilkins, 2011: 404). In other words, accountability has increased as a feature of education since the 1980s and all school pupils since have encountered teachers working in this system.

The then Children, Schools and Families Committee (2010) argued that accountability is required for school improvement and broader outcomes for children:

> *schools should be held publicly accountable for their performance as providers of an important public service. We concur with the views expressed in evidence to us that the two major consequences of the accountability system should be school improvement and improvement in broader outcomes for children and young people, including well-being.*

(Children, Schools and Families Committee, 2010)

Connecting education to the wider aims of society is both problematic and useful when thinking about professionalism. It has been argued that professionals should play an important role in shaping society and this altruism helps set professionals apart from other occupations (Carr, 2000). If a primary teacher is able to shape the lives of young people, they are also shaping broader society by influencing the citizens of the future. However, to hold teachers accountable for broader outcomes can also be problematic as there are aspects of children's lives that sit outside teachers' control. For example, a teacher may teach effectively in a morally acceptable manner and therefore provide a good education to the children in their class. Yet, a child who is encountering a challenging home life may find that the work of the teacher is undone by other social and cultural circumstances. The teacher is still able to account for their actions (i.e. justify what they have done to try to support individual children), but this does not eradicate the possibility that a child could still decline in terms of their broader outcomes and well-being. It has been seen how politicians and the media will often suggest that teachers and schools should be held account for broader issues in society. For example, following a series of riots that occurred in 2011, London's mayor at the time, Boris Johnson, connected the 'nihilism' with poor literacy rates in schools (Winter and Mulholland, 2012). Of course, teachers are key to improving the outcomes for children. However, there are limits to what teachers can achieve. For example, another way to improve the educational outcomes in a society is to find solutions to child poverty: *A strategy of poverty alleviation should form the basis of a holistic programme to improve the attainment of disadvantaged pupils* (Education Policy Institute, 2018: 21). Therefore, primary teachers should recognise how their professional role is to educate children to the best of their ability and how their relationships with children can make a positive difference, but also recognise that there are many other professional occupations that are required to make a fully functioning society.

WHAT IS THE RELATIONSHIP BETWEEN ASSESSMENT AND ACCOUNTABILITY?

Statutory assessments feature heavily as part of school accountability. The extent to which assessment data are used to hold schools to account is variable depending on how data are used and published. The following assessment points will be implemented across a primary school:

- EYFS Profile: At the end of reception, the EYFS profile summarises whether each child has met or exceeded expectations against the Early Learning Goals. Reception teachers will also produce a description of children's communication and language development, physical development and personal and emotional development.

- Phonics Screening Check: At the end of Year 1, children are assessed on their ability to decode words. This test may be repeated in Year 2 for children that did not pass the test in Year 1.

- Key Stage 1 National Curriculum Tests: At the end of Year 2, children will take tests in reading and maths. These tests are sometimes referred to as SATs. The tests complement teacher assessments that also include writing. It is a statutory requirement for schools to take part in external moderation of teacher assessment.

- Multiplication tables check: At the end of Year 4, children may take a times tables test to check their understanding.

- Key Stage 2 National Curriculum Tests: At the end of Year 6, children will take tests in reading, grammar, punctuation and spelling and mathematics. Writing assessments are submitted based on teacher assessment and subject to the same statutory moderation arrangements as in Key Stage 1.

Schools submit assessment results to the government. Depending on how schools are structured (e.g. through a trust or local authority), governing bodies and local bodies may also expect to see the results. For example, in an academy trust data may be submitted to trust managers so they can compare performance between schools and target resources or support. When a school is visited by Ofsted, inspectors will want to see all the data available for current and past cohorts in school.

Some data sets, such as the phonic screening check results, are not published externally. These results will be used locally by the school but may also be used by local governing bodies to hold the school to account. Other data sets are used as part of the school performance profile. The performance profile is published externally and can be used by anyone who wants to compare one school to another. All primary schools can be found and compared at the following government website: https://www.compare-school-performance.service.gov.uk/

THEORY FOCUS NEOLIBERALISM, TESTING AND THE MARKETISATION OF PRIMARY EDUCATION

Neoliberalism is an ideology that features prominently within the public sector in England. It is the belief that public sector institutions will be more efficient and likely to improve if they are placed in a competitive environment. The instruments of school league tables and Ofsted reports, for example, enable parents, as consumers, to choose the school that they want their children to attend. Schools that are sought after and seen to be successful will benefit in the marketplace; schools that are not effective will not be sought after by their communities and, in theory, will be driven to raise standards and improve their position in the market. The reality of this is somewhat different as there are other factors that determine whether a parent, if viewed as a consumer, can make choices about the school for their child. For example, house prices close to a successful school are likely to be higher than house prices close to schools that are less successful (DfE, 2017a), and this is just one example of how choice is impacted by the consumer's cultural, social and economic capital.

Neoliberalism commodifies learning; for primary schools, the test results become the commodity that can be marketed towards others:

> test scores have always been important for schools to demonstrate at a general level how effective they are as institutions. However, prior to the current highstakes, high-accountability testing regime in an education market, such assessment outcomes were essentially a public good. Such goods have two features: they are nonexcludable, meaning that the benefit they offer is, at least to some extent, for everyone; and they are non-rivalrous, meaning that their 'consumption' by any one party (the school perhaps) does not prevent their use by another. As the market model has taken hold over the last 30 years, placing schools in competition with each other, so the public goods of pupil outcomes have become private goods for schools, owned exclusively by them for their own use and rivalrous in the way they are 'consumed' in the service of the competitive market environment.
>
> (Pratt, 2016: 897)

Neoliberalism also impacts what is taught in schools and how it is taught. For example, comparable test results place an emphasis on English and maths in primary schools. What constitutes knowledge within the curriculum is equally influenced by what can be compared and marketised. Even evidence-based practice is influenced by the marketisation of education:

> the idea that teachers should learn and use evidence-based best practice, and be held accountable for it, under the system of indirect surveillance. The evidence base appealed to is provided by the testing system, via an international literature (now very large) of correlational studies on what variables are associated with improved test results. The abstracted 'teacher effectiveness' literature is a striking example of the technicization of knowledge.
>
> (Connell, 2013: 109)

Therefore, the route to school improvement can be packaged through evidence-informed practices that are aligned to a narrow set of instruments for school success. When being held to account, successful teachers may be those who are able to replicate expected teaching practices and produce the desired results in those subjects that are the focus of assessment frameworks. Teachers who are less successful may be equally well-intentioned but unable to demonstrate what is required in a neoliberal system. This does not necessarily mean that the system needs to be overhauled, but it does highlight the way that accountability needs to be understood within a wider societal acceptance of neoliberal ideals.

WHAT IS THE ROLE OF SCHOOL INSPECTION?

School inspection has long been a feature of education in England. The first two inspectors that held the title 'Her Majesty's Inspectors' were appointed under Queen Victoria in 1839. Although education and inspection have seen many changes since, it was not until 1992 that revolutionary change of the inspection system took place (Thomas, 1998). The 1992 Education (Schools) Act led to the creation of Ofsted as a non-ministerial department. The creation of Ofsted was set against the backdrop of the then Prime Minister, John Major's, 'Parent's Charter':

> inspection was henceforth to act on behalf of the consumer, as a 'regulator' of standards and quality. Thus HMI would have to accept new responsibilities to parents as well as to the Secretary of State, and would need to rethink their relationship with schools.
>
> (Cunningham, 2012: 102)

The role of a non-ministerial department is to report to government while being independent of it. This distinction is important as Ofsted should feel free to challenge and question government policy if their findings suggest that it is not working on the ground. In addition to inspecting schools, they also make judgements on Early Years settings, child services, foster and adoption agencies, initial teacher education and further education establishments. The work undertaken by Ofsted is transparent, which means that anyone can view an inspection report for any setting that has been visited.

Modern-day professions, particularly those that are subject to public spending, are similarly subject to regulation. The Care Quality Commission, for example, is an independent regulator that, among other things, provides judgements on the quality of hospitals in England. However, the place of external regulation can sit uncomfortably with traditional definitions of professional occupations. Evetts (2009) suggests that the rise of organisational professionalism is a result of the new-managerialism in public services. This form of professionalism requires externalised forms of regulation. The alternative, 'occupational professionalism', is one where the professional institutions and associations help practitioners to control their own work. This can be seen through the efforts of the Chartered College of Teaching, which is a member-led association with an aim to raise the status of the teaching profession.

In the past, an implication of Ofsted has been that the teaching profession have adapted their curriculum, pedagogy and assessment in ways that are perceived to be 'Ofsted approved'. For example, schools have been reported to dedicate staff-meeting time towards watching Ofsted-judged 'Outstanding' lessons and dissecting them into a tick-list of ingredients that should be replicated in teaching (Stone, 2020). Such practice is concerning when examined through the lens of professionalism, as it can be seen as eroding professional autonomy. Furthermore, primary pupils are *not standardized; thus effective practice cannot be reduced to routines* (Darling Hammond, 2013: 126). Even evidence-informed practice requires teachers to exercise their professional judgement and be reflexive to move children forward in their learning. As a response to the concerns that Ofsted has given rise to a 'preferred' approach in school, the regulator produced a 'myth-busting' document, that among other things, emphasised that *Ofsted doesn't prescribe any particular teaching style* (Ofsted, 2019).

— CLASSROOM LINKS ————————————————————

Consider what you know about effective teaching practice. Make a list of strategies that you believe teachers should use on a regular basis. These can be linked to a subject, or could be about general primary classroom practice.

How do you know that these strategies are effective?

If you can attribute research and evidence to the strategies, then there are likely to be empirical foundations for your approach. For example, if you list systematic synthetic phonics as the approach that you will take for reading, then there are research papers that argue the effectiveness of this approach.

If you are not sure why some of the strategies on the list are effective, it could be that these are strategies learnt through first-hand experience in the primary school environment. For example, you may learn that counting from five down to one in order to gain children's attention is a behaviour management strategy that works because you have seen other teachers using the strategy and achieved a relatively high success rate when replicating that strategy for yourself.

If you have strategies on the list that you use because others have told you that it should be done that way, this is where some further criticality may be beneficial. If you are told that 'Ofsted expects it to be done like this', then it is worth exploring where the evidence for this claim exists. It may be that there is an Ofsted research report that signposts effective practice. However, if it is based on anecdotal evidence of what one inspector has deemed to be effective, then teachers should be wary.

HOW ARE INDIVIDUAL TEACHERS HELD TO ACCOUNT?

Whether training to teach, completing induction or working as a fully qualified teacher, teachers will need to demonstrate that they meet the Teachers' Standards. In order to support their progress, trainees or practising teachers will engage in any combination of the following:

- be observed by a mentor or senior leader;

- submit their pupils' work for quality assurance, moderation and scrutiny;

- submit progress data for their pupils;

- engage in professional review meetings to discuss improvements to practice;

- share lesson planning with senior colleagues or mentors for feedback;

- produce written reports and/or summaries of evidence.

The activities above are both supportive and ways that teachers can be held to account. Trainee teachers will begin to become accountable for the progress of children that they teach. The activities listed above can be supportive in helping the teacher make progress and also ensure that children continue to make progress while the trainee teacher is practising. Qualified teachers engage in an annual cycle of performance review or appraisal that can also make use of the activities above. The annual review meeting is an opportunity for the teacher to celebrate their successes across the year, but also a chance for supportive conversations about future development. Across the year, at different review points, a teacher's line manager may want to observe lessons, look at pupils' work, or scrutinise performance data in order to ensure the teacher is on course to meet their targets.

Teachers' performance appraisal targets are likely to be linked to the school's own targets as set out in their improvement plans. Improvement plans are an important aspect of school accountability and will be shared within localised frameworks (for example, improvement plans may be shared with governing bodies). If a school has a target to raise standards in reading, then it is likely that this target will be shared among the teaching staff. However, the National Education Union (2019) argues against the use of numerical objectives as children's performance in tests can be affected by other variables outside the teacher's control. They argue for objectives to be Specific, Measurable, Achievable, Relevant and Time-bound (SMART targets).

— CLASSROOM LINK

Consider the following target, taken from the National Education Union:

- develop strategies to increase opportunities for reading for pleasure to improve reading skills for your pupils, and begin to assess their impact.

Compare this with a target linked to numerical performance:

- ensure that 80 per cent of children meet age-related expectations for reading in the end-of-year summative tests.

Does the shift in language between the targets shift the way that you would teach, or the curriculum decisions that you will make? Does the shift in language between the targets influence conceptions of professionalism for the primary teacher?

WHY SHOULD PROFESSIONAL TEACHERS BE WARY OF PERFORMATIVE PRACTICES?

When tasked to meet named objectives, there is a possibility that the focus on the objective leads to a loss of focus on another task. One consequence of the target-driven culture of the 2000s and 2010s was that it led to performative practices in some schools:

[Performativity] alludes to the work that performance management systems do on the subjectivities of individuals … Performativity is enacted through measures and targets against which we are expected to position ourselves, but often in ways that also produce uncertainties about how we should organise ourselves within our work.

(Ball, 2008: 51)

Performativity can alter the decision-making of a teacher or the way that they carry out their role. It can occur when teachers want to be seen to be doing something that they think others are expecting of them, even if this is contrary to what they believe they should be doing: *Schooling thus demands of teachers engagement in a doxa of performativity in which they must do accountability work; that is, they must act in particular ways that are valued within the school system and make these visible to others* (Pratt, 2016: 896).

For example, in the 2000s and 2010s, the drive to raise standards in English and maths, led to the narrowing of the curriculum in many primary schools. Therefore, in some cases, children were being denied a broad and balanced curriculum because schools needed to be seen to be driving up standards in the core subjects. This does not mean that teachers believe that the arts or humanities are of less importance; it occurred because the measurement of a school's success was presented through league tables of National Curriculum Tests in core subjects. Ofsted also had a part to play in this performativity culture, as recognised by the chief inspector:

> *For a long time, our inspections have looked hardest at outcomes, placing too much weight on test and exam results when we consider the overall effectiveness of schools. This has increased the pressure on school leaders, teachers and pupils alike to deliver test scores above all else.*
>
> (Spielman, 2018)

Subsequently, the framework for inspection has been written with a stronger emphasis on the whole of the primary school curriculum. This may be seen as welcomed by many in the profession, but an emphasis on a broad and balanced curriculum should be achieved because those in the profession believe it to be integral to their aims and not because this is the new focus from Ofsted.

As professionals paid from public taxation, it is important that primary teachers are held to account for the outcomes in the classrooms and the decisions that they make. An element of this will always require acquiescing to the expectations of others. In particular, it can be argued that primary school teachers work collectively to uphold the reputation of the school. They have a professional obligation to teach the children, thus improving individual children's outcomes. However, if they do this effectively and in a morally acceptable manner then they will also contribute to the reputation of the school overall. Parents will be aware of the schools in their communities that are sought after, oversubscribed when it comes to admissions and spoken of favourably. They will also be aware of the schools that have a bad reputation, schools that parents avoid listing for school admissions and are spoken of less favourably. Cribb (2009) suggests that modern-day professional cultures require an element of impression management through paying attention to public image and investing time in public relations. Therefore, the success of an individual teacher may only be viewed through the success of the school as a whole. For example, Troman et al. (2007: 562) argue that 'middle class' parents are often the ones that are *demanding performance from the school in terms of test scores*. A Year 6 teacher who may be accountable for the outcomes in National Curriculum Tests could find themselves focused on managing the external expectations placed upon the school and need to reconfigure their professionalism as a result.

Accountability can be easier for a teacher working within a school where the school's professional culture is aligned with the teacher's own professional expectations and values. However, where a teacher is expected to perform in ways that do not align with their own beliefs, it can lead to 'values schizophrenia':

A kind of values schizophrenia is experienced by individual teachers where commitment, judgement and authenticity within practice are sacrificed for impression and performance. Here there is a potential 'splitting' between the teachers' own judgements about 'good practice' and students' 'needs' and the rigours of performance.

(Ball, 2003: 221)

Such tensions between values can create a dilemma in the classroom.

CLASSROOM LINK

Consider the type of teacher that you are when being observed by a mentor or senior colleague. Does your teaching change? Is the effort put into planning and preparation greater when there is a known observation? Would the children notice a difference in your practice?

It is a natural response for a teacher to want to give a good impression. However, if a teacher invests greater energy and time into a lesson to please the observer we should ask why the same energy and time has not gone into preparing lessons for the children at other times. This commonplace scenario goes some way to explain issues around performativity. We begin to see how making a good impression can become more important than the children's learning, albeit in a time-limited way. Children in the observed lesson may be taught better than usual because the teacher has 'pulled out all the stops', but if this is not consistent with the teacher's typical practice then what was the point of 'pulling out all the stops'? Arguably, the teacher has prioritised their own need to impress a senior colleague in this instance. In other words, even if the secondary beneficiaries are the children, who may learn more effectively, the principal purpose was not for their benefit but for the teacher.

Studies into teachers' professional identities, such as Brown and Manktelow, highlight how professionalism has shifted as a result of the standards agenda. They find that teachers will accommodate the *social pressures of accountability* (2015: 78), but also define their own measures of success that are separate to the measures that are used to hold teachers publicly accountable such as SATs and league table positions. It is therefore important for early career teachers to consider their own motivations in the primary classroom and how they will use this to define their professional identity.

WHAT HAPPENS IF PRIMARY TEACHERS ARE NOT PROFESSIONAL?

As this book is focused on professionalism, it is worth highlighting how primary teachers are held accountable if they are not able to uphold professional standards of behaviour and conduct. All schools have a complaints procedure and a set of internal disciplinary processes. It is important that these procedures are followed if a complaint is made against a teacher, whether by a parent, pupil, member of staff, or member of the wider community. Typically, this would involve an internal investigation, although outside advice can be sought by the investigator in required. If the investigation reveals that the conduct is serious enough, it can be passed onto the government's Teacher Regulation Agency to decide whether it is necessary to convene a teacher misconduct panel. The teacher misconduct panel members review the case, ask the teacher to account for their actions and ultimately decide whether there has been:

- unacceptable professional conduct;

- conduct that may bring the profession into disrepute;

- a conviction, at any time, of a relevant criminal offence.

If applicable, a prohibition order can be applied that prevents the teacher working in schools again.

Without question, the seriousness of professional misconduct should be realised by anyone working in education. In particular, it is worth considering how a teacher's misconduct can bring the profession into disrepute. Part Two of the Teachers' Standards requires teachers to uphold public trust in the profession. The public must trust that schools are safe spaces for children and fulfilling their role in the wider societal context. Even though teacher misconduct is rare compared with the total population of school teachers, it is imperative that all teachers consider how they uphold standards in public life. Teaching as a profession is only as successful as the sum of its parts.

CHAPTER SUMMARY

What does it mean to be accountable as a primary school professional?

In the English education system, as in other countries, accountability is high stakes for primary teachers. As a teaching profession, there are wider societal expectations that must be upheld. This chapter has invited primary professionals to consider:

- how primary teachers are accountable within their local school structures and how the school is accountable within broader society;

- the role that Ofsted plays in holding schools to account;

- how accountability can lead to performativity practices.

ASSIGNMENT LINKS

Within assignments for teacher education programmes it will be important to demonstrate criticality. Assignments linked to English and mathematics assignments may require the use of national test data to support arguments about teaching within these subjects. Academic arguments will be strengthened by considering the broader philosophical positioning of these subjects and the neo-liberal ideology that underpins wider societal expectations for standards to be raised. Therefore, as part of any critical analysis, it is worth considering what is being measured, why it is being measured and whether a child who does not perform well against the given metrics could still be classed as achieving within the subject if assessment was looked at differently.

━━━━━━━━━ **FURTHER READING** ━━━━━━━━━

Much of the work of Stephen Ball considers the effects of neoliberal ideology on schools. A starting point could be:

Ball, S. (2017) *The Education Debate* (3rd edn). Bristol: Policy Press

The Education Debate *explores the neoliberal context that professional teachers encounter, along with the policy technologies that reinforce the model of schooling that is experienced. The accountability agenda can be best understood in relation to this broader context.*

BIBLIOGRAPHY

Abbott, A. (1988) *The System of Professions: An Essay on the Division of Expert Labour*. Chicago: University of Chicago Press.

Almond, M. (2004) Drama. *English Teaching Professional*, *35*: 7.

Almond, M. (2019) *Putting the Human Centre Stage: Practical Theatre Techniques to Develop Teacher Presence, Rapport and a Positive Classroom Community*. Brighton: Pavilion.

Amabile, T. and Kramer, S. (2011) *The Progress Principle: Using Small Wins to Ignite Joy, Engagement, and Creativity at Work*. Boston, MA: Harvard Business Review.

Ball, S. (2003) The teacher's soul and the terrors of performativity. *Journal of Education Policy*, *18*(2): 215–28.

Ball, S. (2008) Performativity, privatisation, professionals and the state. In Cunningham, B. (ed.), *Exploring Professionalism*. London: Bedford Way Papers.

Ball, S. (2017) *The Education Debate* (3rd edn). Bristol: Policy Press.

Beijaard, D. (2019) Teacher learning as identity learning: models, practices, and topics. *Teachers and Teaching*, *25*(1): 1–6.

BERA (2014) *Research and the Teaching Profession: Building the Capacity for a Self-Improving Education System*. London: BERA.

Bérci, M. E. (2006) The *staircase* of teacher development: a perspective on the process and consequences of the unity and integration of self. *Teacher Development*, *10*(1): 55–71.

Bergviken Rensfeldt, A., Hillman, T. and Selwyn, N. (2018) Teachers 'liking' their work? Exploring the realities of teacher Facebook groups. *British Educational Research Journal*, *44*(2): 230–50. Available at: https://doi.org/10.1002/berj.3325. Accessed 16 February 2021.

Beverton, S. (2006) Collaborating with parents. In Arthur, J., Grainger, T. and Wray, D. (eds), *Learning to Teach in the Primary School*. Abingdon: Routledge.

Biesta, G., Priestley, M. and Robinson, S. (2015) The role of beliefs in teacher agency. *Teachers and Teaching*, *21*(6): 624–40.

Brien, A. (1998) Professional ethics and the culture of trust. *Journal of Business Ethics*, *17*(4): 391–409.

Brown, Z. and Manktelow, K. (2015) Perspectives on the standards agenda: exploring the agenda's impact on primary teachers' professional identities. *Education*, 3–13, *44*(1): 68–80.

Bruner, J. S. (1971) *The Process of Education* revisited. *Phi Delta Kappan*, *53*(1): 18–21.

Bruner, J. S. (2009) *The Process of Education*. Cambridge, MA: Harvard University Press.

Bubb, S. and Earley, P. (2010) *Helping Staff Develop in Schools*. London: SAGE.

Cambridge International Dictionary of English (1995) Cambridge: Cambridge University Press. Online: https://dictionary.cambridge.org/. Accessed 4 January 2021.

Campbell, E. (2003) *The Ethical Teacher*. Maidenhead: Open University Press.

Carpenter, J. and Harvey, S. (2020) Perceived benefits and challenges of physical educators' use of social media for professional development and learning. *Journal of Teaching in Physical Education*, *39*: 434–44. Available at: https://doi.org/10.1123/jtpe.2020-0002. Accessed 15 February 2021.

Carr, D. (2000) *Professionalism and Ethics in Teaching*. London: Routledge.

Carr, D. and Skinner, D. (2009) The cultural roots of professional wisdom: towards a broader view of teacher expertise. *Educational Philosophy and Theory*, *41*(2): 141–54.

Chappell, C. (2003) *Reconstructing the Lifelong Learner*. Abingdon: Routledge.

Children, Schools and Families Committee (2010) *School Accountability: Conclusions and Recommendations*. Available at: https://publications.parliament.uk/pa/cm200910/cmselect/cmchilsch/88/8803.htm. Accessed 28 February 2021.

Coe, R. (2013) Improving education: a triumph of hope over experience. *Inaugural Lecture of Professor Robert Coe, Durham University*, 18 June. Essay version available at: https://profcoe.net/publications. Accessed 25 June 2021.

Coe, R., Aloisi, C., Higgins, S. and Major, L. E. (2015) *What Makes Great Teaching? Review of the Underpinning Research*. London: Sutton Trust.

Connell, R. (2013) The neoliberal cascade and education: an essay on the market agenda and its consequences. *Critical Studies in Education*, *54*(2).

Cranefield, J. and Yoong, P. (2009) Crossings: embedding personal professional knowledge in a complex online community environment. *Online Information Review*, *33*(2): 257–75.

Cranston, J. (2011) Relational trust: the glue that binds a professional learning community. *Alberta Journal of Educational Research*, *57*(1): 59–72.

Cribb, A. (2009) Professional ethics: whose responsibility? In Gewirtz, S. Mahony, P., Hextall, I. and Cribb, A. (eds), *Changing Teacher Professionalism: International Trends, Challenges and Ways Forward*. Abingdon: Routledge.

Crome, S. and Cise, R. (2020) Rethinking teacher wellbeing. *Impact: Journal of the Chartered College of Teaching*, 9. Available at: https://impact.chartered.college/article/rethinking-teacher-wellbeing/. Accessed 5 January 2021.

Cuddy, A. (2015) *Presence: Bringing your Boldest Self to your Biggest Challenges*. London: Hachette.

Cunningham, P. (2012) *Politics and the Primary Teacher*. London: Routledge.

Danielson, A. and Warwick, P. (2014) 'All We Did was Things Like Forces and Motion …': multiple discourses in the development of primary science teachers. *International Journal of Science Education*, *36*(1): 103–28.

Danielson, C. (2007) *Enhancing Professional Practice: A Framework for Teaching* (2nd edn). Alexandria, VA: ASCD.

Darling-Hammond, L. (2013) Teaching and the change wars: the professionalism hypothesis. In Wise, C., Bradshaw, P. and Cartwright, M. (eds), *Leading Professional Practice in Education*, London: Open University Press.

Davidson, K. and Case, M. (2018) Building trust, elevating voices, and sharing power in family partnership. *Phi Delta Kappan*, *99*(6): 49–53.

Day, C. (2004) *A Passion for Teaching*. London: Psychology Press.

Day, C. (2020) How teachers' individual autonomy may hinder students' academic progress and attainment: professionalism in practice. *British Educational Research Journal*, *46*(1): 247–64.

Day, C., Sammons, P., Stobart, G., Kington, A. and Qing, G. (2007) *Teachers Matter: Connecting Lives, Work and Effectiveness*. Maidenhead: Open University Press.

Department for Education (DfE) (2011) Teachers' Standards: Guidance for school leaders, school staff and governing bodies. Available at: https://assets.publishing.service.gov.uk/government/uploads/system/uploads/attachment_data/file/665520/Teachers__Standards.pdf. Accessed 28 February 2021.

Department for Education (DfE) (2013) National Curriculum in England: Primary curriculum. Available at: https://www.gov.uk/government/publications/national-curriculum-in-england-primary-curriculum. Accessed 28 February 2021.

Department for Education (DfE) (2014) Promoting fundamental British values as part of SMSC in schools. Available at: https://assets.publishing.service.gov.uk/government/uploads/system/uploads/attachment_data/file/380595/SMSC_Guidance_Maintained_Schools.pdf. Accessed 1 March 2021.

Department for Education (DfE) (2017a) House prices and schools: do houses close to the best performing schools cost more? Available at: https://assets.publishing.service.gov.uk/government/uploads/system/uploads/attachment_data/file/600623/House_prices_and_schools.pdf. Accessed 28 February 2021.

Department for Education (DfE) (2017b) Statutory Framework for the Early Years Foundation Stage. Available at: https://www.foundationyears.org.uk/files/2017/03/EYFS_STATUTORY_FRAMEWORK_2017.pdf. Accessed 25 June 2021.

Department for Education (DfE) (2018) Health and safety: responsibilities and duties for schools. Available at: https://www.gov.uk/government/publications/health-and-safety-advice-for-schools/responsibilities-and-duties-for-schools. Accessed 28 February 2021.

Department for Education (DfE) (2019a) Initial teacher training core content framework. Available at: https://assets.publishing.service.gov.uk/government/uploads/system/uploads/attachment_data/file/919166/ITT_core_content_framework_.pdf. Accessed 1 March 2021.

Department for Education (DfE) (2019b) Teacher workload survey 2019. Available at: https://assets.publishing.service.gov.uk/government/uploads/system/uploads/attachment_data/file/855933/teacher_workload_survey_2019_main_report_amended.pdf. Accessed 28 February 2021.

Department for Education (DfE) (2019c) The Early Career Framework. Available at https://assets.publishing.service.gov.uk/government/uploads/system/uploads/attachment_data/file/913646/Early-Career_Framework.pdf. Accessed 1 February 2021.

Department for Education (DfE) (2020a) School teachers' pay and conditions document 2020 and guidance on school teachers' pay and conditions. Available at: https://www.gov.uk/government/publications/school-teachers-pay-and-conditions. Accessed 28 February 2021.

Department for Education (DfE) (2020b) School workforce statistics 2020. Available at: https://explore-education-statistics.service.gov.uk/find-statistics/school-workforce-in-england. Accessed 25 June 2021.

Department for Education (DfE) (2021a) Keeping children safe in education. Available at: https://www.gov.uk/government/publications/keeping-children-safe-in-education--2. Accessed 28 February 2021.

Department for Education (DfE) (2021b) What maintained schools must publish online. Available at: https://www.gov.uk/guidance/what-maintained-schools-must-publish-online. Accessed 31 March 2021.

Department for Education/Department of Health and Social Care (DfE/DHSC) (2015) Special educational needs and disability code of practice: 0 to 25 years. Available at: https://www.gov.uk/government/publications/send-code-of-practice-0-to-25. Accessed 28 February 2021.

Dewey, J. (1933) *How We Think*. New York: Buffalo Press.

Dweck, C. (2015) Carol Dweck revisits the growth mindset. *Education Week*, *35*(5): 20–4.

Education Endowment Foundation (2021) Evidence summaries. Available at: https://educationendowmentfoundation.org.uk/evidence-summaries/. Accessed 1 March 2021.

Education Policy Institute (2018) Education in England: Annual Report 2018. Available at: https://epi.org.uk/wp-content/uploads/2018/07/EPI-Annual-Report-2018-Executive-Summary.pdf. Accessed 28 February 2021.

Education Support (2020) Teacher Wellbeing Index 2020. Available at: https://www.educationsupport.org.uk/resources/research-reports/teacher-wellbeing-index-2020. Accessed 28 February 2021.

Elton-Chalcraft, S., Revell, L. and Lander, V. (2018) Fundamental British values. In Cooper, H. and Elton-Chalcraft, S. (eds), *Professional Studies in Primary Education* (3rd edn). London: SAGE.

Evetts, J. (2009) New professionalism and new public management: changes, continuities and consequences. *Comparative Sociology*, 8: 247–66.

Firth, J. (2017) What is evidence-based education? Available at: https://www.jonathanfirth.co.uk/blog/evidence. Accessed 5 January 2021.

Firth, J. (2018) Experts in learning. In Rycroft-Smith, L. and Dutaut, J. L. (eds), *Flip The System UK: A Teachers' Manifesto*. Abingdon: Routledge.

Freidson, E. (2001) *Professionalism: The Third Logic*. Chicago: University of Chicago Press.

Frost, D., Ball, S. and Lightfoot, S. (2018) The HertsCam network: supporting non-positional teacher leadership. In Rycroft-Smith, L. and Dutaut, J. L. (eds), *Flip The System UK: A Teachers' Manifesto*. Abingdon: Routledge.

Gilroy, P. (2018) Preface: securitisation and values. In Lander, V. (ed.), *Fundamental British Values*. Abingdon, Oxfordshire: Routledge.

Glazzard, J. and Mitchell, C. (2018) *Social Media and Mental Health in Schools*. St Albans: Critical.

Goodson, I. F. and Cole, A. L. (1994) Exploring the teacher's professional knowledge: constructing identity and community. *Teacher Education Quarterly*, 21(1): 85–105.

Guerriero, S. (2014) Teachers' pedagogical knowledge and the teaching profession background report and project objectives. *Paper presented at OECD symposium Teachers as Learning Specialists – Implications for Teachers' Pedagogical Knowledge and Professionalism, Belgium*, 18 June. Available at: http://www.oecd.org/education/ceri/background_document_to_symposium_itel-final.pdf. Accessed 1 February 2021.

Halstead, M. and Pike, M. (2006) *Citizenship and Moral Education: Values in Action*. London: Routledge.

Hart, R. (2007) Act like a teacher: teaching as a performing art. Doctoral dissertation, University of Massachusetts.

Hayes, D. (2012) *Foundations of Primary Teaching*. Abingdon: Routledge.

Helsby, G. and McCulloch, G. (1996) Teacher professionalism and curriculum control. In Goodson, I. and Hargreaves, A. (eds), *Teachers' Professional Lives*. London: Falmer.

Her Majesty's Government (2011) Prevent strategy. Available at: https://assets.publishing.service.gov.uk/government/uploads/system/uploads/attachment_data/file/97976/prevent-strategy-review.pdf. Accessed 1 March 2021.

Holland, D., Lachicotte Jr, W., Skinner, D. and Cain, C. (1998) *Identity and Agency in Cultural Worlds*. Cambridge, MA: Harvard University Press.

Home Office (2019) Revised Prevent duty guidance: for England and Wales. Available at: https://www.gov.uk/government/publications/prevent-duty-guidance/revised-prevent-duty-guidance-for-england-and-wales. Accessed 2 February 2021.

Hoyle, E. (1974) Professionality, professionalism and control in teaching. *London Educational Review*, 3(2): 13–19.

Hoyle, E. (2008) Changing conceptions of teaching as a profession: personal reflections. In Johnson, D. and Maclean, R. (eds), *Teaching: Professionalization, Development and Leadership*. Dordrecht: Springer.

Hudson, B. (2008) A didactical design perspective on teacher presence in an international online learning community. *Journal of Research in Teacher Education*, 15(3–4): 93–112.

Jackson, P., Boostrom, R. and Hansen, D. (1993) *The Moral Life of Schools*. San Francisco: Jossey-Bass.

Keenan, J. (1996) *Virtues for Ordinary Christians*. London: Sheed and Ward.

Korthagen, F. A. (2004) In search of the essence of a good teacher: towards a more holistic approach in teacher education. *Teaching and Teacher Education*, 20(1): 77–97.

Kounin, J. S. (1970) *Discipline and Group Management in Classrooms*. New York: Holt McDougal.

Lander, V. (2016) Introduction to fundamental British values. *Journal of Education for Teaching*, *42*(3): 274–9.

Laxton, D. (2020) A parent's guide to promoting early learning and development at home (0–5 years): supporting families during the coronavirus pandemic. *SKIP for Early Years Educators*. Available at: https://www.skipforeyeducators.co.uk/booklet/covid19_familybooklet.pdf. Available at: 10 October 2020.

Lee, S. (1962) Amazing Fantasy #15. *Marvel Comics Group*. Available at: https://www.marvel.com/comics/issue/16926/amazing_fantasy_1962_15. Accessed 18 June 2021.

Lexico (2021) Networking. Available at: https://www.lexico.com/definition/network Accessed 1 March 2021.

Lowman, J. and Lowman, J. (1984) *Mastering the Techniques of Teaching* (Vol. *1990*). San Francisco: Jossey-Bass.

MacIntosh, D. (2014) *Ethical Culture: Building a Culture of Integrity*. London: Chartered Insurance Institute.

Marcia, M. and Garcia, I. (2016) Informal online communities and networks as a source of teacher professional development: a review. *Teaching and Teacher Education*, *55*: 291–307. Available at: https://www.sciencedirect.com/science/article/pii/S0742051X1630021X?via%3Dihub. Accessed 16 February 2010.

Maslach, C. and Leiter, M. P. (2016) Understanding the burnout experience: recent research and its implications for psychiatry. *World Psychiatry: Official Journal of the World Psychiatric Association (WPA)*, *15*(2): 103–11.

Meijer, P. C., Korthagen, F. A. and Vasalos, A. (2009) Supporting presence in teacher education: the connection between the personal and professional aspects of teaching. *Teaching and Teacher Education*, *25*(2): 297–308.

Monbiot, G. (2019) The new political story that could change everything. *TedSummit*. Available at: https://www.ted.com/talks/george_monbiot_the_new_political_story_that_could_change_everything. Accessed 25 June 2021.

Muckenthaler, M., Tillmann, T., Weiß, S. and Kiel, E. (2020) Teacher collaboration as a core objective of school. *School Effectiveness and School Improvement: An International Journal of Research, Policy and Practice Development*, *31*(3): 486–504.

National Education Union (NEU) (2019) Setting appraisal objectives: NEU guidance. Available at: https://neu.org.uk/advice/setting-appraisal-objectives-neu-guidance. Accessed 26 February 2021.

National Education Union (NEU) (2020) Directed time and how to tackle workload in your school. Version 2. Available at: https://neu.org.uk/media/11391/view. Accessed 28 February 2021.

NHS England (2020) Gender identity development service for children and adolescent service specification. Available at: https://www.england.nhs.uk/wp-content/uploads/2017/04/gender-development-service-children-adolescents.pdf. Accessed 28 February 2021.

Noddings, N. (2003) Is teaching a practice? *Journal of Philosophy of Education*, *37*(2): 241–51.

NSPCC (2021) Protecting children from radicalisation. Available at: https://www.nspcc.org.uk/keeping-children-safe/reporting-abuse/dedicated-helplines/protecting-children-from-radicalisation/ Accessed 28 February 2021.

OECD (2018) Valuing our teachers and raising their status: how communities can help. International Summit on the Teaching Profession. Available at: https://www.oecd.org/education/valuing-our-teachers-and-raising-their-status-9789264292697-en.htm. Accessed 25 June 2021.

Ofsted (2019) Education inspection framework. Available at: https://www.gov.uk/government/publications/education-inspection-framework/education-inspection-framework. Accessed 25 June 2021.

Patel, P. (2019) Decolonise the curriculum. *TED Talk*. Available at: https://www.ted.com/talks/pran_patel_decolonise_the_curriculum. Accessed 25 June 2021.

Pollard, A. (2014) *Reflective Teaching in Schools* (4th edn). London: Bloomsbury Press.

Poore, M. (2015) *Using Social Media in the Classroom: A Best Practice Guide*. London: SAGE.

Pratt, N. (2016) Neoliberalism and the (internal) marketisation of primary school assessment in England. *British Educational Research Journal, 42*(5): 890–905.

Prestridge, S. (2019) Categorising teachers' use of social media for their professional learning: a self-generating professional learning paradigm. *Computers and Education, 129*: 143–58. Available at: https://www.sciencedirect.com/science/article/pii/S0360131518303002. Accessed 6 January 2020.

Race, R. (2020) Repositioning curriculum teaching and learning through Black-British history. Available at: https://www.bera.ac.uk/publication/repositioning-curriculum-teaching-and-learning-through-black-british-history. Accessed 28 February 2021.

Rodenburg, P. (2007) *Presence*. London: Penguin.

Rodgers, C. R. and Raider-Roth, M. B. (2006) Presence in teaching. *Teachers and Teaching: Theory and Practice, 12*(3): 65–287.

Roeser, R. W, Skinner, E., Bears, J. and Jennings, P. A. (2012) Mindfulness training and teachers' professional development: an emerging area of research and practice. *Child Development Perspectives, 9*(2): 167–73.

Roness, D. (2011) Still motivated? The motivation for teaching during the second year of the profession. *Teaching and Teacher Education, 34*(1): 349–67.

Ryan, R. M. and Deci, E. L. (2000) Self-determination theory and the facilitation of intrinsic motivation, social development, and well-being. *American Psychologist, 55*(1): 68–78.

Santiago, R., Garbacz, A., Beattie, T. and Moore, C. (2016) Parent–teacher relationships in elementary school: an examination of parent-teacher trust. *Psychology in the Schools, 53*(10): 1003–17.

Scharmer, C. O. (2016) *Theory U: Learning from the Future as it Emerges* (2nd edn). San Francisco: Berrett-Koehler.

Schon, D. (1987) *Educating the Reflective Practitioner*. San Francisco: Jossey-Bass.

Shulman, L. (1986) Those who understand: knowledge growth in teaching. *Educational Researcher, 15*(2): 4–14

Shulman, L. (1987) Knowledge and teaching foundations of the new reform. *Harvard Educational Review, 57*(1): 1–23.

Shulman, L. S. and Shulman, J. H. (2007) How and what teachers learn: a shifting perspective. *Journal of Curriculum Studies, 36*(2): 257–71.

Skaalvik, E. M. and Skaalvik, S. (2014) Teacher efficacy and perceived autonomy: relations with teacher engagement, job satisfaction and emotional exhaustion. *Psychological Reports, 114*: 68–77.

Smith, G. and Smith, S. (2013) From values to virtues: an investigation into the ethical content of English primary schools assemblies. *British Journal of Religious Education, 35*(1): 5–19.

Spielman, A. (2018) HMCI commentary: curriculum and the new education inspection framework. Available at: https://www.gov.uk/government/speeches/hmci-commentary-curriculum-and-the-new-education-inspection-framework. Accessed 28 February 2021.

Stevenson, H. (2018) Flip the system? Get organised! In Rycroft-Smith, L. and Dutaut, J. L. (eds), *Flip The System UK: A Teachers Manifesto*. Abingdon: Routledge.

Stone, G. (2012) Ethics, values and the teacher. In Knowles, G. and Lander, V. (eds), *Thinking Through Ethics and Values in Primary Education*. London: SAGE/Learning Matters.

Stone, G. (2020) Narratives of early career teachers in a changing professional landscape. In Parsons, J. M and Chappell, A. (eds), *The Palgrave Handbook of Auto/Biography*. London: Palgrave.

Stone-Johnson, C. (2014) Parallel professionalism in an era of standardisation. *Teachers and Teaching: Theory and Practice, 20*(1): 74–91.

Sullivan, L. E. (2009) *The SAGE Glossary of the Social and Behavioral Sciences*. Available at: https://sk.sagepub.com/reference/behavioralsciences/n17.xml. Accessed 25 June 2021.

Tauber, R. T. and Mester, C. S. (2007) *Acting Lessons for Teachers: Using Performance Skills in the Classroom* (Vol. *38*). Westport, CT: Greenwood.

Thomas, G. (1998) A brief history of the genesis of the new schools' inspection system. *British Journal of Educational Studies, 46*(4): 415–27.

Thompson, J. G. (2018) *The First-Year Teacher's Survival Guide: Ready-To-Use Strategies, Tools and Activities for Meeting the Challenges of Each School Day*. Hoboken, NJ: John Wiley & Sons.

Tour, E. (2017) Teachers' self-initiated professional learning through personal learning networks. *Technology, Pedagogy and Education, 26*(2): 179–92. Available at: https://doi. 10.1080/1475939X.2016. 1196236. Accessed 16 February 2021.

Trent, J. (2014) 'I'm teaching, but I'm not really a teacher'. Teaching assistants and the construction of professional identities in Hong Kong schools. *Educational Research, 56*(1): 28–47.

Troman, G., Jeffrey, B. and Raggl, A. (2007) Creativity and performativity policies in primary school cultures. *Journal of Education Policy, 22*(5), 549–72.

Trust, T. (2012) Professional learning networks designed for teacher learning. *Journal of Digital Learning in Teacher Education, 28*(4): 133–8.

UNICEF (1990) The United Nations Convention on the Rights of a Child. Available at: https://www.unicef.org/child-rights-convention/convention-text. Accessed 25 June 2021.

Voisin, A. and Dumay, X. (2020) How do educational systems regulate the teaching profession and teachers' work? A typological approach to institutional foundations and models of regulation. *Teaching and Teacher Education, 96*: 103–44.

Wenger, E. (1998) *Communities of Practice: Learning, Meaning, and Identity*. Cambridge: Cambridge University Press.

Weston, D. and Clay, B. (2018) *Unleashing Great Teaching*. Abingdon: Routledge.

Wiliam, D. (2018) *Creating The Schools Our Children Need: Why What We're Doing Now Won't Help Much (And What We Can Do Instead)*. West Palm Beach: Learning Sciences International.

Wilkins, C. (2011) Professionalism and the post-performative teacher: new teachers reflect on autonomy and accountability in the English school system. *Professional Development in Education, 37*(3): 389–409.

Wilkinson, D. (2016) The use of questions in primary science: a collaborative action research study. Doctoral thesis, University of Southampton, School of Education.

Winter, P. and Mulholland, H. (2012) Boris Johnson says poor schools helped cause riots. *Guardian*. Available at: https://www.theguardian.com/politics/2012/mar/23/boris-johnson-bad-schools-london-riots. Accessed 28 February 2021.

Wyse, D. (2002) *Becoming a Primary School Teacher*. Abingdon: Routledge.

INDEX

CPSIA information can be obtained
at www.ICGtesting.com
Printed in the USA
JSHW040302240522
26087JS00003B/89